D0118325

Writing Whizardry

60 Mini-lessons to Teach Elaboration and Writer's Craft

Maity Schrecengost

MAUPIN
HOUSE

Writing Whizardry
60 Mini-lessons to Teach Elaboration & Writer's Craft

Maity Schrecengost
©2001 Maity Schrecengost

Cover design: Maria Messenger
Layout design: Hopper Graphics

Library of Congress Cataloging-in-Publication Data

Schrecengost, Maity, 1938-
    Writing whizardry : 60 mini-lessons to teach elaboration and writer's craft / Maity Schrecengost.
        p. cm.
    Includes bibliographical references and index.
    ISBN 0-929895-45-2
        1. English language--Composition and exercises--Study and teaching (Elementary) 2. English language--Composition and exercises--Study and teaching (Middle school) I. Title.

LB1576 .S3265 2001
372.62'3044--dc21   00-054890

ISBN-10: 0-929895-45-2
ISBN-13: 978-0-929895-45-1

10 9 8 7 6 5 4

Other books by Maity Schrecengost
    Voice Whizardry
    Tasso of Tarpon Springs
    Panther Girl
    Research to Write
    Researching Events
    Researching Issues
    Researching People
    Write to be Read

Maity Schrecengost is an author and educational consultant based in Florida.
Contact her through the publisher for inservice training and conference speaking.

The author extends a great big thanks to the young writers listed in order of appearance of work included in this handbook.

Jenna Johnson	Natalie Lopez	J. T. Linde
Stephenie Schauberger	Sarah Schmitt	Brandon Rickrode
Sarah Smith	Rebekah Frazee	

Maupin House Publishing, Inc.
2416 NW 71st Place
Gainesville, FL 32653
1-800-524-0634
www.maupinhouse.com

Publishing Professional Resources that Improve Classroom Performance

This one is for Nancy, Laura, and Pat —
team supreme!
I love you guys!

• • •

Table of Contents

Reproducibles and Transparency Masters 95

Reproducibles

Transparency Masters

Author and/or Illustrator Videos

Recommended for Your Professional Library

Bibliography

About the Author

Other Maupin House Resources

Introduction

The greatest challenge intermediate-grade teachers face is how to teach children to write elaboratively. Other than writing e-mail messages, letters, memos, and, of course, never-ending lesson plans, most teachers, however, are not themselves writers. In fact, I have found in talking with teachers that few have even been exposed to writing instruction beyond that for preparing college or university papers. Even then, the instruction may have been limited to writing format with little, or no, emphasis given to graceful elaborative writing.

No wonder many teachers feel a bit daunted by the task of teaching the literary devices, composing skills, and techniques that will make their students' writing clear, interesting and exciting to read!

Teachers know graceful elaborative writing moves writing assessment scores to higher levels. They want to know how to present lessons that teach elaboration and writing craft. They want lessons that provide opportunities for practice. Even more importantly, they want to know these lessons will carry over to children's own work, that they will result in quality writing that earns high scores on writing assessment tests— scores for which teachers are being held accountable.

A tall order? Yes! But, here's good news! *Writing Whizardry* helps transform budding writers into writing whizzes.

How the Handbook is Organized

We tend to group writing into two classifications for middle-grade writers: narrative, writing to tell a story; and expository, writing to explain, which includes persuasive writing. This classification is helpful for teaching composing structure.

Children need to recognize that narrative writing generally involves telling a story that takes place over a period of time, has characters and setting, and may involve a conflict or problem to be solved. Narrative writing may be fiction, (The Invisible Student) or non-fiction (Our Class Trip to NASA).

Expository writing is non-fiction and is used to present information for the purpose of explaining (Flying is a Great Way to Travel), instructing (How to Make a Model Airplane), convincing (Everyone Should Practice Conservation) or imparting information (Australia's Amazing Animals).

Although the basic structure of narrative and expository writing is different, elements of expository writing may be found in narratives and narratives may be embedded in an expository piece.

The writer may use exposition within the narrative to explain events or set forth facts relative to the narrative. For example, when writing a narrative about a class trip to NASA, the writer might *explain* that NASA stands for National Aeronautic Space Administration. Or he might explain the training an astronaut undergoes in preparation for space missions.

Short narratives may be used in expository writing to provide examples to support an idea. In an expository piece about why flying is a great way to travel, the writer might include a short vignette (narrative) *telling* about the first time she flew in a plane.

Skills for effective writing between narrative and expository writing carry over, too. Specificity of word choice, supporting details, focus, and making transitions are just as important in narrative writing as in expository. By the same token, expository writing should be as inventive and colorful in presentation as narrative writing. Expository is not synonymous with boring! The use of sensory words, metaphorical language, and colorful examples add excitement to the expository piece.

Because elements of expository writing may be found in narratives and narrative elements in expository, I have not organized the mini-lessons in narrative and expository groupings. Good writing is good writing. In most cases both narrative and expository examples are included in the mini-lesson.

Organization of the Mini-lessons

Within a typical classroom, students are found of varying writing abilities. By the intermediate grades many children are at the apprentice level, although some third graders may still be beginning, or novice, writers. Most fourth and fifth graders are apprentice, or developing, writers, with a few able students working at an advanced, or more proficient level.

These mini-lessons progress from the more basic to the more complex. Early mini-lessons are appropriate for both novice and apprentice writers. Most of the lessons are for apprentice writers, while the final mini-lessons are directed to the more advanced writers in your classroom. A few of the lessons at the end of the handbook are more suitable primarily for awareness. Use these lessons to introduce a literary device, but don't expect students to use the device consistently, if at all, in their own compositions.

Because of the wide range of student ability within a typical classroom, you may choose to use some of the mini-lessons for small group instruction. Others lend themselves to whole-class instruction. All are designed to fit within your writing workshops or classes.

While all the mini-lessons lead to more elaborative writing, they fall into two general categories: elaboration and writer's craft. To help you identify where each mini-lesson fits, icons are used. Mini-lessons that are elaborative are identified by (*E*); writer's craft mini-lessons by (*WC*).

You will recognize that some of the mini-lessons seem to repeat, or echo, prior lessons. This is deliberate. In some cases, the mini-lesson takes an earlier lesson to a higher level. In others, the concept is presented from a different angle or within a different context. Because elaborative writing is developed with lots of practice over time, all of the mini-lessons may be repeated with increasingly good results.

Each mini-lesson is introduced with an explanation of the concept that will be taught. I include **non-examples** (writing that doesn't work well) and **examples** (writing that works), suggestions for teaching the lesson, and ideas for **extending the lesson.** Throughout the handbook, you will find **Tips** for effective teaching.

Many of the mini-lessons include a bibliography of children's literature that illustrate the mini-lesson skill. Several of the mini-lesson skills are so consistently found in quality children's literature, a bibliography listing of examples is unnecessary. In a few cases, I have listed children's textbooks which provide additional instruction in the skill.

The mini-lessons will, I'm sure, inspire you to create additional lessons and examples of your own. Space is provided with each mini-lesson for your notes, observations, and lesson extensions.

At the end of the handbook is a section with masters of lengthy mini-lesson examples for reproducibles and overhead transparency masters. You'll also find listings of various additional resources. These items are referenced in the text .

How to Use This Book

· · · ·

You can work through the handbook, presenting the lessons in the order given, providing the children with a sequence of lessons moving from basic to more sophisticated skills. But, you also can select mini-lessons that address weaknesses you observe in your students' writing as they work toward developing writing proficiency. This works well in classrooms with a wide range of skill levels or to address genre-specific skills. Or, you may choose to select mini-lessons that fit well with other aspects of your language arts program. If, for example, you are focusing on characterization in reading, mini-lessons 18 - 25 will fit nicely with your reading curriculum.

Teachers using the mini-lessons in *Writing Whizardry* have found that the lessons and practices not only teach desired skills but are so much fun the children beg for more.

The mini-lessons in *Writing Whizardry* are designed to help you transform your students into elaborative, effective writers. I think you will find as you use the handbook that you, too, will enjoy learning more about the excitement and rewards of the writing craft.

Writing Craft

Writing *is* craft. As with any other craft, there are skills and techniques to be learned, practiced, and honed to perfection. To accomplish this, of course, takes time. Lots of it. Professional writers spend many, many years learning their craft. Yet some teachers, perhaps in response to over-burdened curriculums, expect students to be able to perfect their craft by writing to an occasional, perhaps only weekly (or, sadly, even less often!), prompt with little, or no, prior instruction in the techniques and devices for successful composition.

Many teachers of writing, including myself, find that writing is best taught in workshop or studio situations at regularly scheduled times. In a writing workshop, children are free to explore, experiment, and try various writing techniques. And because children know writing is going to happen at regularly designated times, they are able to engage in pre-writing. In other words, they're able to think about writing and plan for it. Children often tell me that their best planning times for what they will write are just before they fall asleep at night.

During these regularly scheduled writing workshops, students and teacher write together, writing craft is modeled, work is shared, risk-taking is encouraged, and children have the time they need to practice and hone their writing skills.

Many fine books have been written for teachers with valuable suggestions for creating a writing climate in the classroom. They suggest using mini-lessons during writing workshop as an effective tool for instructing both beginning and apprentice writers.

Focusing on the Elements of Writing

Mini-lessons presented during a writing workshop may take several forms. They may be **procedural**, during which the teacher presents the structure of the class, procedures to be followed for sharing, storing, and publishing work, classroom management, and/or the procedures for storage and use of writing materials.

Or the lessons may deal with **mechanics or conventions**. The focus of these lessons is to provide instruction in grammar, punctuation, capitalization, and other commonly accepted conventions of written language.

Finally, the mini-lessons may focus on **elements of writing**. These mini-lessons teach beginning writers the techniques all writers, novice and professional, use to produce effective writing. The secrets of the trade, so to speak.

Much has been written about management of the writing classroom—and we know procedures will differ from classroom to classroom. Few teachers find teaching mechanics and writing conventions problematical. But many teachers, especially those who are not themselves practicing writers, struggle with how to teach the craft of writing. The mini-lessons in *Writing Whizardry* focus on elements of writing — the writing craft — and how to teach it.

A teacher can't simply *tell* the children a writer's technique, — for example, "Writers need to use strong verbs," —and expect to see that technique carried over in the students' writing. Students need to *see* the writing *happening* (teacher modeling), **understand** *how and why* the techniques work, and *have frequent opportunities to **practice*** what they're learning. In other words, writing must be presented as any other content area subject, such as reading, math, or social studies.

Writing Content

In some classrooms, writing is treated as an "extra" — as something to fit in if time permits or as a "fill-in" activity when there's time left over. This approach serves only to convey the dreadful message that "writing isn't important."

In such classrooms, writing topics may be pulled from so-called "story starter boxes" or from a list of suggested topics that do not allow students to engage in topic selection. Learning to choose and focus on a topic is central to learning to write well. There are, of course, times when "writing on demand" or "deadline writing" is required, but most of a young writer's practice should be on self-selected topics.

In classrooms where writing is treated as an "extra," students may be instructed to write to the "prompt" with no opportunity to engage in pre-writing information gathering activities. Often, little or no modeling of writing or instruction in the craft of writing precedes the writing activity. Additionally, the children's work may be turned in for immediate teacher evaluation allowing no time after the writing for sharing and/or peer critiquing, and revision. Amazingly, teachers in these classrooms bewail the fact that their students' writings never seem to improve!

For children to achieve optimum success in writing, writing must be seen as an integral part of the curriculum. Sometimes I hear teachers claim they "don't have time to teach writing." To those teachers, I say, "You don't have time to *not* teach writing." Because writing teaches kids critical thinking and organizational skills that carry over to every other subject, the teaching of writing should be an integral part of every elementary school curriculum.

I ask teachers to consider this question once posed by writing guru, Donald Graves: "You can teach reading without teaching writing, but can you teach writing without teaching reading?" Obviously the answer is, "No." As children learn to compose, they are also learning important reading skills: main idea, sequencing, supporting details, author's intent, organizing information, characterization, cause and effect, metaphorical language, and so on. Reading and writing go hand-in-hand.

Being able to process information in print, reorganize the information, and express understandings with clarity in one's own language is a necessary skill in all subject areas.

The Writing Notebook

To emphasize that writing is a content-area subject, like reading, math, or social studies, children in many classrooms keep writing notebooks. I prefer to have them use composition books with marbleized covers and sewn-in pages. The hard cover helps set the notebook apart from others they may have in their desks and the sewn-in pages discourage tearing

TIP

Enthusiasm is contagious. Help your students "catch" the writing fever. Show your own delight over a well-turned phrase or share your excitement when you read a strong passage.

pages out. The notebooks stay intact, like a text book. In fact, the writing notebook *becomes* their textbook!

Early in the year, explain how the notebooks will be used. Stress that these notebooks are one of the most important things the children will use all year and , if they keep them carefully, they will continue to use the lessons they contain all the rest of their school years. And, trust me, they will. It never fails to thrill me when high school, and even college, students approach me in the grocery store or on the street and relate to me a success they have had in writing, concluding by saying, "And it all started with you in fourth grade!" Talk about music to a teacher's ears!

How to Use the Notebooks

The writing notebooks are working textbooks. They are used for recording writing mini-lessons as they are taught and for practicing the skills taught in the mini-lessons. Because the notebooks are used for practice, the samples of student work taken from the notebooks for inclusion in *Writing Whizardry* are not edited and may have spelling and/or mechanical errors.

My students did not use the notebooks for their self-selected "works-in-progress" topics or assigned writings. Those works were dated and stored in personal writing folders. About midway through the school year, these folders got quite "fat". At that time, we began to use two folders for each child: one for *finished works*, and another for *works in progress*. Although I spot-checked the notebooks daily to be sure each child was on task and making progress, I did *not* grade the notebooks or use them for evaluation purposes. Rather, after several days (or weeks) of incorporating a group of mini-lessons into the writing workshops, I took a writing sample from each child.

When evaluating the sample, one of the things I looked for was the effective use of skills taught during the mini-lessons. At this stage in the writing process, when work was submitted for evaluation, I expected the piece to have been self-edited and to be as error-free as each child could make it.

After introducing and stressing the importance of the writing notebooks, have the children write on the inside front page the words *Writing Notebook*, their name, and the school year. This makes the book "official." Some students choose to divide their notebooks into sections for different writing genres.

From this point on, students date each entry and state the topic of the lesson. Write the topic on the board or chart paper for the children to copy. You may prefer to use an overhead projector. Often I state the topic in sentence form, for example: "Good writers use strong verbs." I may simply use a label, "Strong Verbs". Or, to elaborate on the idea of verbs needing to be strong enough to do the job, I may have fun using a catchy title like, "Put Muscles in Your Verbs."

TIP

Writing workshops are not necessarily democratic. Children are not always treated in the same way, in that expectations for individual students may differ. Acceptable work among young writers may differ quite a bit. Once a student demonstrates mastery of a skill, it is fair to expect consistent use of that skill in his or her work.

Some children enjoy drawing a cloud around the topic. As time goes by, I find the children become quite creative with the use of colored pencils in making clouds, underlining things they want to remember, and starring to emphasize writing of which they are particularly proud. In addition to inviting the children to star anything they were proud of, I asked them to mark work they especially wanted me to see. At the end of writing workshop, they put their notebooks, open to the marked passages, on the conference table where I could then read the indicated sections and respond with comments in the margin. The notebooks become highly individual. In essence, the children are writing their own textbooks! And that, to me, is more than a little exciting.

A note about spelling: In the early days of writing process, the term "invented spelling" came into vogue. Its intent—to encourage kids to "keep-on-writing" without getting bogged down in the "how-do-you-spell?" syndrome—was good. But, the term suggests that one can "invent," or create, new ways of spelling.

I prefer the use of the terms "predictive," "approximate," or "temporary" spelling. Kids predict in reading, estimate (or approximate) in math, and predict hypotheses in science, so they are familiar with the terms. They know a prediction or approximation may not be correct and that a revision may be needed "after all the facts are in." "Temporary" suggests that the spelling isn't permanent, it's "only for now." Encouraging "predictive," "approximate," or "temporary" spelling during early drafts lets kids write without breaking the flow of ideas, but still know that revisions to correct the spelling may be necessary at the point of publishing (making the piece available for others to read).

TIP

Word banks of frequently-used or often-misspelled words help beginning writers, especially if the banks include blank space for students to add their own "spelling demons."

The writing notebooks become individualized text books that each student writes for himself.

Teaching the Mini-lessons

Present the Lesson

Because children need to be able to identify what doesn't work as well as what does work in writing, begin each lesson with a *non-example* — a sample of a sentence or group of sentences that is not effective. Write the non-example on the board or overhead transparency and ask the children to copy the non-example in their notebooks. For instance, you might write the sentence: *John ran around the track.*

Even though *John ran around the track* is an O.K. sentence and the words do express a complete thought, point out that *ran* is a weak verb. It doesn't really do the job. The verb needs muscles! Encourage the children to brainstorm words that would be more effective.

Challenge the children to think of words that more accurately convey meaning by asking questions like, "How might John *run* if he is a long distance runner?" "Or how might John *run* if he's running from the class bully?" "What if John is the guy next door who runs every morning for exercise?" As the children brainstorm, list their sentences with the better verb choices on the board as the children copy them in their notebooks.

Practice the Lesson

After the children have a variety of sentences listed, ask them to practice writing sentences of their own. Their notebooks might then look something like this:

Good Writers Use Strong Verbs

Non-example: John ran down the street.

Example: *John jogged down the street.*
              John raced down the street.
              John flew down the street.
              John sprinted down the street.

Practice: John trotted around the track.
              John. . .

After students have had time to practice the skill, you might play a game. For this lesson, for example, write a weak verb on the board and have the children copy the verb in their notebooks. Their next job is to write beside it a stronger verb. Several children may be asked to share a verb they have written, and the rest of the children can add those words to their notebooks. Then, write another weak verb and repeat the process, keeping up a brisk pace. To vary the game, you may have the children suggest "weak" verbs themselves and then work together to brainstorm stronger ones.

Apply the Learning

Finally, have students take out a piece they have been working on. Ask them to examine their work and find at least one verb they can change to a stronger one. Several children should be given the opportunity to **share** the changes they have made and **tell how** the change makes their writing better. In this way, students transfer the learning to their own writing.

Each of the 60 mini-lessons follows the same basic format. A mini-lesson taught during writing workshop may take anywhere from ten to twenty minutes—including time for the children to examine and revise their own work—depending on the enthusiasm and learning taking place. Kids get really excited and experience shows that teachers are usually ready to draw the lesson to a close long before the children are!

The mini-lessons in *Writing Whizardry* have been used in classrooms with intermediate-grade students. First, the lesson is explained. Then the lesson topic is stated, and **non-examples** (samples of writing that doesn't work or do not demonstrate the skill) and **examples** (writing samples that do demonstrate the skill) are given. Additional non-examples are suggested for extending the lesson, as well as samples of possible revisions for more effective writing. Use these revised examples for demonstration when students have difficulty coming up with their own ideas or to clarify the concept. The very best examples in response to the non-examples will, of course, come from the children themselves as they practice and internalize the skills.

Remember that the writing you do often seems to "just appear." Children need to see writing happening. They need to see the writing process in action. Familiarize yourself with the mini-lesson beforehand, so that when the kids watch as you write the non-examples on the chalkboard or overhead transparency, it will appear to them to be as spontaneous as possible. Then, let them in on your thinking as you say things like, "Hmmmm - this verb *ate* doesn't really show how Danny ate when he was in a hurry to go out and play. What if I used *gobbled* instead?" Then line out the word ate and write gobbled in above it.

Danny ate gobbled his breakfast.

As the children listen to you think aloud and watch you make changes, they will begin to be able to transfer the learning to their own writing—an immediate learning tool. As they record and practice the mini-lessons in their notebooks, the mini-lessons become a resource for students to review skills long after the lesson is complete.

TIP

Don't neglect the sharing time! The kids love it, they learn from each other, and the enthusiasm generated is phenomenal!

Why Do The Mini-lessons Work?

At least nine predictors of a successful writing program have been identified. Looking at these predictors, you can easily see how mini-lessons fit into and support a well planned writing curriculum.

Predictability - Knowing that writing is going to happen and knowing when it will happen enables children to engage in pre-writing. Kids also need to be able to predict *how* writing will happen. The mini-lessons follow a format that children quickly become comfortable with. They anticipate the non-examples to show them what doesn't work and can count on examples that "show them how to do it." In addition, they know that each mini-lesson affords them opportunities to practice and transfer the learning to their personal writing.

Ownership - The very best demonstration of writing ownership is one I heard Donald Graves use many years ago. He compared ownership of writing with the difference between renting a house and owning one. When something goes wrong, he said, renters simply "call the landlord." They trust the landlord will maintain the property. They are not interested in painting or landscaping the property themselves. Owners, on the other hand, are eager to make improvements, to invest time and energy to improve the value of their property. Children who only *rent* their writing from the teacher-landlord are less likely to be willing to make an investment. They happily hand it in to let the teacher "fix it." When children *own* their writing, it becomes very important to them. They want to make the writing the best it can be.

Mini-lessons help give children ownership of their writing as they create their own text-books, compose examples to demonstrate good writing techniques, and incorporate those techniques into their own works-in-progress.

Self-selected topics - Writers write best about things they know about, want to know about, or have an emotional investment in. In writing workshops, most of the children's writing time should be spent on topics they have selected. The mini-lessons enable children to apply skills they have learned from modeling, direct instruction, and practice to their own works in progress.

Structure - Children - perhaps all writers — need a structured situation in which they have freedom to explore, create, and take risks. Few writers are able to write in the midst of chaos or uncertainty. As children learn to know what to expect in terms of how the workshop is structured and what is expected of them they are able to grow confidently in writing. Mini-lessons, by their very nature, provide structure to empower learning.

Modeling - Telling students how to write is not enough. Teachers must model writing. Modeling is built into every mini-lesson, giving students first-hand, "how to do it." demonstrations.

Direct Instruction - In the early days of writing process, children wrote freely, but somewhat willy-nilly. It was as though we somehow expected them to pick up successful writing techniques and practices through a vague process of osmosis. We now know that children need to be taught writing content through direct instruction in the skills that lead to clear elaborative writing. The mini-lessons provide clear, easy-to-present, effective guides for instruction.

Conferencing - All writers need response; feed-back to let them know when they have been successful and suggestions for areas of improvement. That's why professional writers join writer's groups. Conferencing—both peer and teacher—is an important element in the mini-lessons and should be utilized often within the context of the writing workshops.

Sharing - Writing is for reading. Writing needs to be shared. What's the point of writing if there is no audience? Unless, of course, you happen to be incredibly introverted or narcissistic! Every mini-lesson has built in opportunities for children to share their writing.

Playfulness - I firmly believe that playfulness is a vital key to the success of any writing program. A grim-as-death, controlling, overly serious atmosphere is sure to squelch even the most enthusiastic writer. Mini-lessons provide opportunities to celebrate successes, to sympathize when something doesn't work while you "dust 'em off and set them back on their feet" to try again, and allow you - and fellow students - to delight in one another's work.

So why do mini-lessons work? Because they embed all nine predictors of a successful writing program.

60
Mini-lessons

Mini-lesson 1
Put Muscles in Your Verbs

Children are still in the process of developing their vocabularies, so verb choice is often limited to common use verbs, like *go, went, ran, said, like,* etc. Point out that verbs are the workers in a sentence, and they have to be strong enough for the task. Mini-lessons that help make children more aware of specific verb choice not only make their writing more lively and exact, they broaden their speaking vocabulary as well.

Non-example:	Danny ate his lunch.
Example:	*Danny gobbled his lunch.*
	Danny nibbled at his lunch.

Susan smiled as she read her book.
Susan (grinned, laughed out loud, giggled, chuckled, chortled) as she read her book.

Alex put his books on the table.
Alex (threw, slammed, dropped) his books on the table.

Lions hunt their prey.
Lions stalk their prey.

Mockingbirds sing like other birds.
Mockingbirds mimic other birds.

"Go away," Josh said angrily.
"Go away," (snarled, growled, muttered, roared) Josh.

TIP

Throughout the day, take every opportunity to call the children's attention to strong verbs when they appear in their reading texts, read aloud time, content area texts, and (even more fun) daily conversations.

Strong verbs don't need adverbs! For example, *angrily* is not necessary in the sentence above if a stronger verb is used. The reader will know Josh is angry from the verb used. This is an excellent opportunity to introduce the use of a thesaurus, a book of synonyms and antonyms.

Resources

Schiller, Andrew & Jenkins, William A. *In Other Words: A Beginning Thesaurus.* New York: Lothrop, Lee, and Shepard Company, 1978.

Urdang, Laurence. *A Basic Dictionary of Synonyms and Antonyms.* New York: Elsevier/Nelson Books, 1978.

Witlels, Harriet & Greisman, Joan. *The Clear and Simple Thesaurus Dictionary.* New York: Grosset & Dunlap, 1971.

Witlels, Harriet and Greisman, Joan. *A First Thesaurus.* New York: Golden Book, 1985.

Mini-lesson 2
Say What You Mean!

Children tend to be non-specific in their writing, using generic words such as *store, town, street*, rather than specific nouns, including proper nouns. Specificity in writing answers *who, what,* and *where* questions in the reader's mind. Children need plenty of opportunities to practice replacing non-specific nouns in their writing with specific words. Remind your budding writers to tell their readers *exactly* who, where, and what they are referring to in their piece.

TIP

After this mini-lesson, be sure to have the children examine previous writing for places where they have used non-specific nouns. This is also a good time to "tuck in" a lesson on capitalizing proper nouns.

Non-example: We went to the store for ice cream.
                    who   where   what

Example: *Mom and I went to Publix Market for Breyer's chocolate chip ice cream.*

                  The kids went to the park to play games.
                  Joe, Sal, and Mary Ann went to Greenfield Park to play soccer.

                  He ate breakfast before he left for the game.
                  Pete drank juice and ate scrambled eggs and toast before he left for the softball game.

                  My school is the best school in town.
                  Park Avenue School is the best school in Newtonville.

                  We went to a professional baseball game at a big stadium.
                  We saw the Pirates play the Red Sox at Three Rivers Stadium in Pittsburgh.

I often demonstrate this lesson by holding up a pencil and saying, "This is a thing I write with." I then hold up a pen and repeat, "This is a thing I write with." Finally, I hold up a piece of chalk and say, "I write with this thing." I point out to the children that in each case they knew what the "thing" was because they could see it. But, if they read a sentence that merely said, "I write with a thing," they wouldn't have a clue what the "thing" was. Demonstrating this difference between oral and written language helps children grasp the need for specificity in writing.

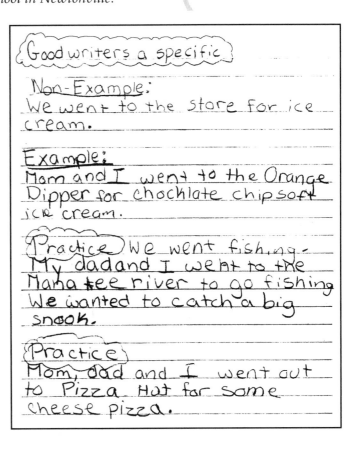

Good writers a specific

Non-Example:
We went to the store for ice cream.

Example:
Mom and I went to the Orange Dipper for chochlate chip soft ice cream.

Practice We went fishing.
My dad and I went to the Mahatee river to go fishing. We wanted to catch a big snook.

Practice
Mom, dad and I went out to Pizza Hut for some cheese pizza.

Mini-lesson 3
Tell It All!

Because the scene or event is so vivid in the writer's own mind, beginning writers often fail to adequately describe it for the readers. A process of subtraction and compression takes place between experiencing an event, telling about it, and, later, writing to describe the event. At the time of experiencing, details are clear and vivid. Later, in relating the event orally, some parts of the experience will have faded and details will be left out. Still later, when writing to tell about the event, even more details and images will be omitted. Mini-lessons such as this one help young writers remember to include enough information to let the reader fully experience the scene or event they are writing about.

Non-example:	Our neighbors bought a car.
Example:	*The Smiths, our next door neighbors, bought a shiny red Ford convertible.*
	It's a nice day.
	Sunlight sparkles on the leaves, a gentle breeze blows, and birds sing in the trees.
	I have a favorite place to read.
	I love to curl up in the big overstuffed chair in the corner of our family room with a good book.
	My little sister is a real pest.
	My kid sister is forever getting into my things with her grubby little fingers.

Relating an experience (say, a birthday party) from a kid's point of view is a fun way to introduce this mini-lesson. Be sure to include all the fun and crazy details that would be vivid in a child's mind. Then, retell the story the way the child would tell his mom about the party when he got home, leaving out many of the fun details. Finally, write on the board the way he would write about the story in school the next day. Something like this: *I went to Jimmy's birthday party. We played games. He got lots of presents. We ate cake and ice cream. It was fun.* (Sound familiar?)

Resources

Christelow, Eileen. *What Do Authors Do?* New York: Clarion Books, 1995.

Tresselt, Alvin. *White Snow, Bright Snow.* New York: Lothrop, Lee & Shepard Co., 1947.

Van Allsburg, Chris. *Jumanji.* Boston: Houghton Mifflin Company, 1981.

Fitzpatrick, Marie-Louise. *The Long March.* Oregon: Beyond Words Publishing, Inc. 1998.

TIP

Have young writers close their eyes to picture the scenes in their minds before they begin to write. Allowing the children to pre-write by talking about the event before writing about it helps children "put back" missing information. Peer conferencing for content, when children ask one another questions about what they want to know more about, elicits additional information.

(See "Peer Conference Form," page 97.)

Mini-lesson 4
Invigorate Your Verbs

Beginning writing is often in the passive voice. In the passive form, the subject is the receiver of the action rather than the doer of it. For example, in the sentence, "The dog was struck by the car" *was struck* is a passive construction. "The car struck the dog" would be in the active voice. Because novice writers depend on the use of "to be" verbs - *is, are, was,* and *were* - their writing is likely to be passive. Mini-lessons like these help children to identify passive verb forms and learn to use the active form, which energizes and gives immediacy to their writing.

Non-example: The building was on fire.
Example: *Fire tore through the burning building.*
   Flames scorched the walls of the building.

   We were kept awake by the barking dogs.
   Barking dogs kept us awake.

   Peppy music was played by the band.
   The band played peppy music.

   Holes are dug by armadillos.
   Armadillos dig holes in people's yards.

   Bees are busy all day long gathering nectar.
   Busy bees gather nectar all day long.

Have the children look at one of their "works-in-progress" and circle all the "to be" verbs (is, are, was, were). Challenge them to change as many as they can from passive to active forms.

TIP

Allow several children to share their changes and tell how the alterations helped the writing.

Mini-lesson 5
Paint Vivid Word Pictures

Writers paint word pictures in the mind of the reader, much as an artist paints on a canvas. Artists use color, lines, and shapes while writers use words. This mini-lesson helps the beginning writer learn to use her whole pallet of colorful words. Encourage the children to think of the reader's mind as a blank canvas, just waiting for them to paint upon.

Non-example: Alice was reading in her room.
Example: *Sunlight streamed through the bedroom window as Alice curled up on her flowered bedspread with her favorite book.*

We live in a nice house.
We live in a white frame house with green shutters that sits back from the road on a grassy hill dotted with tall trees.

Our kitchen is a cozy place.
Our cheerful yellow kitchen with fluffy curtains and flowers on the table makes me feel warm and cozy.

The empty house looked scary.
Cobwebs hanging from the broken windows cast shadows on the rickety old porch.

He's a poor old man.
The old man's tattered clothes hung on his skeleton-like frame as he tottered down the street.

I love to introduce this lesson by drawing a very simple sketch like this shown on the chalkboard or on an over-head transparency. Obviously, this drawing is woefully inadequate!

Next, I ask the children to write in their notebooks what they know from the drawing, which, of course, is very little. Then, I slowly begin to add to the sketch while the children observe and attempt to predict what my sketch is about by adding to the sentence, "I know from the picture. . . "

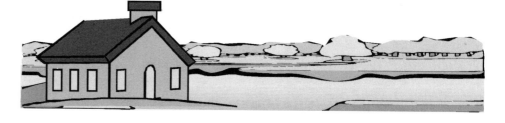

The final detailed sketch may look something like this:

We then talk about how writers need to include enough information in their writing to paint a complete and vivid word picture for their reader-audience.

Resources

Adams, Jeanie. *Going for Oysters.* Illinois: Albert Whitman & Company, 1991.

Auch, Mary Jane. *I Was a Third Grade Science Project.* New York: Holiday House, 1998.

Schrecengost, Maity. *Write to Be Read,* Chapter 12. Wisconsin: Alleyside Press, 1972.

Mini-lesson 6
Fix Your Focus

Beginning writers often lose their focus. (Unfortunately, so do some experienced writers!) They begin writing about one thing, then move on to something else. Soon there may be two or even three stories or main ideas in the piece. Children don't readily see this in their own writing, because to them, everything in their lives is important! That's why we see so many "breakfast to bedtime" stories.

Learning to find the key event, "real story," or main topic, in their piece comes with time after lots of writing experiences. Reading their own work aloud to themselves or to a writing partner helps children learn to identify what their piece is really all about and to recognize where they got off track.

Non-example: One of the most interesting people I know is my grand-mother. She's my dad's mother and she isn't like any other grandmother you've ever known. She lives with my grandfather. He's interesting, too. He served in the Vietnam war. They live on a farm and raise llamas.

Example: *One of the most interesting people I know is my grand-mother. She's my dad's mother and she isn't like any other grandmother you've ever known. She lives on a farm with my grandfather and raises llamas.*

See "Fix Your Focus," page 102.

When you put the non-example on the board or overhead, encourage students to find the place where the piece loses its focus. Point out that although the information about the grandfather is interesting, it detracts from the main idea, or focus, of the paragraph. Perhaps grandfather deserves a piece of his own!

Extending the Lesson

— For practice have the children choose an interesting person they know and write one paragraph about that person. Then, with a partner, ask them to share their work by reading one another's piece aloud to see if they did keep their focus.

— Have the children examine their own works-in-progress and highlight or star where the "real story" begins. In examining the work-in-progress, is there more than one topic? If so, ask the writer which part is most important to her right now. That is the one she should develop.

— Having kids read their work aloud to one another in a "receiving conference" helps students focus their work. During a receiving conference, the partner listens as the writer reads the piece aloud. The conference partner responds to the work by saying, "I heard you say. . .", telling the writer what he or she heard the writer say, using the writer's own words as much as possible. The listener then is able to tell the writer how many topics or main ideas he heard in the piece of writing. More often, the writer is able to identify that there is more than one topic herself.

See "Receiving Conference Form," page 98.

Resources

Christelow, Eileen. *What Do Authors Do?* New York: Clarion Books, 1995.

Roderman, Winifred Ho. *Writing 1: Getting Started*. California: Fearon/Janus, 1990.

Schrecengost, Maity. *Write to Be Read*, Chapter 5. Wisconsin: Alleyside Press, 1992.

Mini-lesson 7
Show - Don't Tell

Beginning writers *tell* their readers. They don't recognize that the same information can be given more interestingly by *showing* the reader what they want him to understand. Showing the reader is accomplished by describing rather than simply stating a fact. Children enjoy "show - don't tell" mini-lessons and are excited when they begin to use and identify examples of "showing the reader" in their own writing.

Non-example:	It's a rainy day.
Example:	*Rain dashed against the windows.*
	Rain drops splashed in the puddles on the street.

The principal is angry.
The principal's eyes flashed as he roared at the kids in the cafeteria.

Lucy is a happy girl.
Lucy skips down the sidewalk, singing as she goes.

It was a pleasant day at the beach.
A cool breeze blew in from the ocean and sea gulls cried overhead.

Cheetahs are pretty and fast.
The swift cheetahs's tawny, black-spotted coat catches your eye.

Remind students about "Show and Tell" days when they brought something they cared a lot about to share with their classmates. Suggest that in writing we are sharing something we care a lot about, too. But, we have to do the showing with our writing.

Demonstrate the difference between "telling" and "showing." Stand before the class, motionless, with a blank expression on your face. In a flat voice, state, "I feel angry." That's telling. Then show anger by stamping your foot while glaring at the children and perhaps yelling. That's showing!

Resources

Byars, Betsy. *Wanted. . . Mud Blossom.* New York: Delacorte Press, 1991.

Ferris, Jeri. *Go Free or Die: A Story about Harriet Tubman.* MN: Carolrhoda Books, Inc., 1988.

Schrecengost, Maity. *Write to Be Read*, Chapter 8. Wisconsin: Alleyside Press, 1992.

TIP

Be sure to allow the children to share their practices. I generally walk around the room as they work and tap children who have written a "super sentence." These children go to the front of the room and share their sentences with the rest of the class. Students work their little hearts out to be ones chosen, they learn from one another, and the enthusiasm generated is incredible!

Mini-lesson 8
Lights! Camera! Action!

Young writers not only tell information (she's a happy girl; it's a rainy day) rather than show the information, they are more apt to name an action than to describe it. Telling the reader what is happening is not nearly as much fun as showing the action. Because kids are by nature active little creatures, they love learning to write to show the action.

Non-example: Tommy acted mad.
Example: *Tommy kicked the chair angrily and stomped out of the room, slamming the door behind him.*

Sally feels sad.
Sally's face crumpled and a tear slid down her cheek.

The teacher is irritable.
Miss Grinch threw her pencil down and said, "Good heavens, why can't you people work quietly?"

The class was in an uproar.
Screaming kids were chasing the fugitive gerbil, knocking papers off the desks, while the teacher yelled, "That's quite enough!"

King snakes suffocate their prey.
King snakes coil around their prey, tightening their coils every time the victim breathes out, until it can no longer take in air.

This mini-lesson takes "show-don't tell" one step further by showing *action* as well as *information*. Demonstrate showing action by first saying, "I cleaned my desk." Now, show cleaning the desk by blowing dust off, stacking papers, gathering up loose odds and ends, etc. Point out that they not only know *wha*t you did, showing tells *how* you did it.

Resources

Burch, Robert. *Ida Early Comes Over the Mountain*. New York: Viking Press, 1980.

Elliott, Leslee. *Really Radical Reptiles and Amphibians*. New York: Sterling Publishing Co., Inc., 1994.

Mini-lesson 9
Set the Scene

The setting of a story may be contemporary, long ago, or even in the future. It may be real-world or fantasy, geographical or historical. The very atmosphere of the story becomes part of the setting. As students learn the importance of settings in the stories they read, they want to give their own stories a time and place to happen.

At this age, children are also learning about cause and effect. The setting of the story has a direct bearing on what can or cannot happen in the story. Make the reading/writing connection by showing students they can't, (as one wrote) "sit down to rest under a palm tree" when they're mountain climbing in the Rockies!

TIP

Venn Diagrams are useful for helping children understand the effect setting has on a story. For example, you might use a Venn Diagram to compare Babe with Babe in the City. How did moving Babe to the city change the characters involved and the plot events?

Non-Example: One day my friend Joey said, "Look what I found."
Example: *The October sun warmed our backs as we dug in the playground sand. Suddenly, Joey said, "Look what I found."*

I walked in the sand.
Coquina shells glistened in the morning sun. Their broken shells hurt my feet as I walked along the shore.

I put my tray down and sat next to Natalie.
Kids' voices, clattering silverware, and the smell of boiled hot dogs filled the cafeteria.

We sat next to a window.
The conductor yelled, "All aboard!" I settled down in my coach seat and rubbed a clean spot on the window to look through as the train pulled out of the station.

I couldn't believe I was seeing all that snow.
Glaciers, pastel colored ice bergs, polar bears. I couldn't believe my eyes. Was I really in Alaska?

Introduce the mini-lesson by discussing the purpose of setting the stage for a play. Talk about what the backdrop provides and why furniture and other props are necessary. Make the analogy between setting the stage for a play and creating a setting for a narrative.

Engage the children in a brainstorming session. Talk about all the times and places a story could happen. Pose questions like: "Could you have a snowball fight in Orlando? Go mountain climbing in Kansas? Take a space flight in 1840?" Stress that readers need to know where and when a story is taking place and that the setting has to be both believable and logical.

Resources

Baum, L. Frank. *The Wizard of Oz*. New York:William Morrow & Co., 1987 Edition. This classic combines both real and fantasy.

Brink, Carol Ryrie. *Caddie Woodlawn*. New York: Simon & Schuster, 1983.

de Angeli, Marguerite. *The Door in the Wall*. New York: Doubleday Books Reissue, 1989.

O'Dell, Scott. *Island of the Blue Dolphins*. Boston: Houghton Mifflin Company, 1960, 1988.

Speare, Elizabeth George. *The Witch of Blackbird Pond*. New York: Houghton Mifflin Company, 1958.

Mini-lesson 10
Exciting Leads

Children need to be shown the importance of starting a piece of writing with a good lead, a beginning that will "lead" the reader right into the story. In narrative writing, a strong lead will include setting, characters, and some indication of what the story is going to be about.

In expository writing, we often call leads a "hook," because of the way they hook the reader and make him or her want to read on. Some of the same elements are at work in expository writing as in narrative writing: catch the reader's attention and let the reader know what the piece is going to be about. The writer often poses a question or makes a startling statement to draw the reader into the piece.

TIP

Draw children's attention at every opportunity to strong leads in their reading books, during read-aloud time, and in the children's recreational reading opportunities.

Non-example: Once there was a Greek boy who wanted to come to America.

Example: *The setting sun spread a golden glow over the deserted market place. Twelve-year old Tasso snatched his red flannel cap from his head as he darted down the cobblestone street. His legs, like pumping pistons, set the tassels of his loose knee-length trousers dancing. Suddenly Tasso stopped short. Loud excited voices from inside the coffeehouse drew him as a flame draws a moth.* (From: *Tasso of Tarpon Springs*, Maupin House, 1998.)

See "Exciting Leads—*Tasso of Tarpon Springs*," page 103.

Point out to students that a good lead will not only catch the reader's attention, it will establish a setting for the story, introduce the main character, and draw the reader into the action by creating tension or posing a question. From clues in the lead in the example, what can the children tell you about where and when the story is taking place? Who do they predict will be the main character? What do they want to know more about?

Non-example: Omri got a weird birthday present.

Example: *It was not that Omri didn't appreciate Patrick's birthday present to him. Far from it. He was really very grateful — sort of. It was, without a doubt, very kind of Patrick to give Omri anything at all, let alone a secondhand plastic Indian that he himself had finished with.* (From *The Indian in the Cupboard.* Lynne Reid Banks, 1980.)

See "Exciting Leads—*Indian in the Cupboard*," page 103.

Non-example: This is a scary story about two kids who go into a spooky house on Halloween.

Example: *Jerry and Karyn's sneakers crunched the dry leaves on the path. "I don't know, Karyn," said Jerry, pushing his mask higher on his nose in order to see better. "It looks scary." Bare tree limbs cast shadows on the gray boards of the rickety old house. Its door, slightly ajar, creaked eerily on rusty hinges.*
*   "Oh, come on Jerry. Don't be such a scairdy-cat," taunted Karyn. "Let's go in. After all, what could possibly happen?"*
*   That's exactly what I'm worried about, thought Jerry.*

See "Exciting Leads—*Scary House Story*," page 104.

Non-example: Once our family went camping out west. It was a real adventure.

Example: *Mom and I unpacked the gear while Dad and Pete put up the tent. A sudden gust of cold wind sent shivers over my bare arms. Mom tossed me a sweatshirt saying, "Even though it's August, it still gets cold this high in the mountains." I smiled happily thinking to myself, "Our Rocky Mountain adventure has begun!" Little did I know.*

See "Exciting Leads—*Camping Adventure*," page 104.

Remind the children that after they have "set the scene" (setting), they want to invite the reader to "come and see the play" (read the story.) If the stage is empty, there's nothing to invite them to, and if the invitation isn't tempting it probably won't be accepted.

Extending the Lesson

— Have the children look at a narrative in progress in their folders. Tell them to read their leads while asking themselves these questions: Is the place where the story is taking place clear? Can the reader tell when the story is happening? Did I introduce the main character? Does the lead pull the reader into the story? Encourage the children to make revisions if the answer to any of the questions is, "No."

Encourage children to rewrite to improve their leads by dividing the class into groups of three for peer-conferencing. Instruct the children to listen for setting, character(s), action, dialogue, and whether the lead makes the reader want to read on. As each writer reads his/her piece, the others in the group will check off each item when they hear it. After allowing time for rewrites, ask each group to choose one person to come forward to share with the whole class.

See "Writing Exciting Leads Peer Conference Form," page 99.

TIP

Demonstrate how leads work by taking a child by the hand and physically pulling the child the direction you want him or her to go. Explain to the children that a lead pulls the reader into the story making him want to read on.

Resources

Avi. *Sore Losers*. New York: Avon Books, 1984.

Keehn, Sally. *I Am Regina*. New York: Bantam Doubleday Books for Young Readers, 1991.

Paulsen, Gary. *My Life in Dog Years*. New York: Bantam Doubleday Books for Young Readers, 1998.

Robinson, Barbara. *The Best Christmas Pageant Ever*. New York: HarperCollins, 1972.

These represent a sampling of a few of my personal favorites. Of course, any well-written children's book will begin with a strong lead.

See "How to Write Exciting Narrative Leads," page 105.

Mini-lesson 11
Grab Your Reader's Attention

Hooks are often used in expository writing. A hook serves essentially the same purpose as a lead. A well-written hook will grab the reader's attention and make him/her want to read on. However, while a lead will often give the reader information in the opening paragraphs about setting, characters, and a hint as to what the story will be about, a hook is more often a short, snappy statement or question used to titillate the reader. Common hooks may be in the form of a question, a short personal anecdote, a quote, a startling statement, or quick visual images.

Non-example: In this piece I will tell you about Florida panthers.

Example: *Have you ever petted a real live panther? I have! And, believe me, it was a thrill! (question)*

In this piece I'm going to tell you why I'd like to visit Australia.

Kangaroos! Koala bears! The Great Barrier Reefs! Crocodile Dundee and the Outback. All these make me long to visit Australia. (quick visual images)

In this piece you will learn some interesting things about Australia.

Kangaroos are road kill in Australia! Read on to learn more interesting facts about the Land Down Under. (startling statement)

I am going to tell you three reasons why I would like to visit Australia.

My friend Jim says that the Great Barrier Reef has some of the most beautiful coral in the world. And he ought to know—he lives in Australia. Which is just one reason why I'd like to visit The Land Down Under. (quote)

If I could visit anywhere in the world, I'd choose Australia. Now I'll tell you why.

All my life I've wanted to see a live kangaroo in the wild Outback of Australia - the Land Down Under. (personal feeling)

Check out a variety of children's periodicals from your media center. Take turns reading the opening sentences from a variety of non-fiction articles. As the passages are read aloud, have the children identify the types of hooks. Have them tell exactly what the writer did to hook the audience.

TIP

All of the non-examples tell the reader what the writer is going to do. Remind the children frequently to not tell their reader what they're going to do — Just Do It!

Extending the Lesson

— Encourage the children to examine their own works-in-progress to determine if they were able to use a "hook."

— Practice writing hooks together as a class activity. Creative, attention grabbing hooks raise scores on expository writing assessments!

Resources

Cobblestone. Peterborough, NH: Cobblestone Publishing Company.

ContactKids. New York: Sesame Workshop.

National Geographic World. Washington, DC: National Geographic Society.

Odyssey Adventures in Science. Petersborough: Cobblestone Publishing Company.

Ranger Rick. VA: National Wildlife Federation.

Elliott, Leslee. *Really Radical Reptiles and Amphibians.* New York: Sterling Publishing Co., Inc. 1994.

See "How to Write Exciting Expository Leads," page 106.

Mini-lesson 12
Satisfying Endings

Just as children have to learn to write strong leads, they also need to learn to write solid, satisfying endings. They have to be shown that writing **The End** at the bottom of the last page does not end the piece. In fact, if they have to tell the reader it's the end, they surely haven't ended the story well.

In narrative writing, a satisfying ending leaves the reader with a sense of completeness, a feeling that there's nothing more to say. The story has been told. There may be unanswered questions, or the ending may leave the reader with the desire for a sequel, but the main story has been told.

In expository writing, the ending should tie all the information together. Commonly used endings include a summary statement, pose a challenge, offer an invitation, or encourage further exploration of the topic.

Higher scores on narrative writing assessment tests require a strong beginning, middle, and ending. If any one of the three is missing, a lower score will result. The ending for an expository piece needs to have a sense of completeness. Both beginnings and endings need to be well developed to earn higher scores.

Non-example: And that's the end.
Example: *Mariah waved as long as she thought he could still see her, then watched as the line of Indians grew faint in the distance. She remembered Daddie calling the removal of the Indians to the West the Trail of Tears. Today, the trail was theirs once more, but the tears were her own.* (From: *Panther Girl,* Maupin House, 1999)

See "Satisfying Endings—*Panther Girl*," page 107.

Although the ending in this example from *Panther Girl,* is bittersweet and leaves the reader wondering if the main characters will ever meet again, the reader knows there's really nothing more to be said.

Non-example: That's the end of my story. "Bye now."
Example: *As Dad put the last of the gear into the van, I stood quietly gazing at the majestic mountains. I wanted to memorize every detail. Our Rocky Mountain Adventure was over. We were going home.*

See "Satisfying Endings—*Camping Adventure*," page 107.

TIP

Be sure to use correct writing terminology. Playful terms like "sloppy copy" convey writing as "kid stuff." Using the terms that "real" writers use, such as "Draft One," or "Rough Draft," lets your student writers know they are learning "real writer's" skills.

I hope you learned something about wood storks.

Now that you've learned about where wood storks live, what and how they eat, why they're important, and how they became an endangered species, I hope you, too, will want to help protect these fascinating birds.

See "Satisfying Endings—*Wood Storks*," page 107.

Select stories the children love and know well and use them as models for satisfying endings. Be sure to read aloud examples of strong expository endings from children's favorite periodicals.

Extending the Lesson

— Have the children look at their own writings to determine if they have ended their own work has a satisfactory ending. If there are loose ends or a sense of incompleteness, have the children rewrite the endings.

See "How to Write Satisfying Narrative Ending," page 108.

See "How to Write Satisfying Expository Ending," page 109.

Resources

Babbitt, Natalie. *Knee-knock Rise.* New York: Scholastic, 1970.

Dahl, Roald. *Charlie and the Great Glass Elevator.* New York: Alfred A. Knopf, 1972.

Fleischman, Paul. *The Half-a-Moon Inn.* New York: Scholastic, 1980.

Paulsen, Gary. *Hatchet.* New York: Simon & Schuster, 1987.

White, E.B. *Charlotte's Web.* New York: Harper and Row, 1952.

Williams, Margery. *The Velveteen Rabbit.* New York: Holt, Rinehart and Winston, 1983.

Use the periodicals listed in Mini-lesson 11 for examples of expository endings.

Mini-lesson 13
Build Bridges

Children often move from one idea to another without giving clues to the reader that time has passed or that a new idea is being introduced. Transitional words and phrases serve as bridges to help the reader make the connections. This mini-lesson provides examples of transitions that move the reader from time to time, place to place, and/or idea to idea.

Non-example: Our teacher, Mrs. Grinch, gave us fifty long division problems for homework. I had to practice the piano after school. We had a soccer game right after dinner. It was really late when the game ended so I didn't have time to do the problems. Mrs. Grinch said, "The first person in each row will collect the homework."

Example: *Our teacher, Mrs. Grinch, gave us fifty long division problems for homework. I had to practice the piano after school. **Then** we had a soccer game right after dinner. It was really late when the game ended, so I didn't have time to do the problems. **The next day**, Mrs. Grinch said, "The first person in each row will collect the homework."*

While Natalie and Jordan were playing pick-up sticks, Natalie's little brother, Davy, snuck up behind them and yelled, "I want to play, too!" causing Natalie to move a stick and lose her turn. "Get out of here and leave us alone!" shouted Natalie. Hearing the commotion from the kitchen, Natalie's mom called out, "Natalie, be nice to your little brother."

Jordan and Natalie sat on the bed planning how to get even.

While Jordan and Natalie were playing pick-up sticks, Natalie's little brother, Davy, snuck up behind them and yelled, "I want to play, too!" causing Natalie to move a stick and lose her turn. "Get out of here and leave us alone," shouted Natalie. Hearing the commotion from the kitchen, Natalie's mom called out "Natalie, be nice to your little brother."

Later, in Natalie's bedroom, *Jordan and Natalie sat on the bed planning how to get even.*

Reading is my favorite subject. I like to read because I can learn about many different places. I loved reading about the Swiss Alps in the book *Heidi*. Reading makes dull days exciting.

Reading is my favorite subject. I like to read because I can learn about many different places. I loved reading about the Swiss Alps in the book Heidi. ***Another reason I like to read is*** *reading makes dull days exciting.*

TIP

For a change of pace, have the kids exchange papers and look for examples of the skill, in this case transitions, used in one another's work. They love to use sticky labels to write positive comments on or simply draw smiley faces to mark the spot!

I also like to read because I can go on adventures with the main characters in the books. So now you know why I like to read.

I also like to read because I can go on adventures with the main characters in the books.

For all these reasons: *because I can learn about new places, make dull days exciting, and go on adventures with the main characters, reading is one of my favorite things to do.*

See "Build Bridges," pages 110-111.

Before showing an example, encourage the children to find the problem in the non-example. Children may not readily see that there is a problem. Learning to recognize problems in the non-examples is a giant step toward being able to see them in their own writing.

Extending the Lesson

— Brainstorm lists of possible transitions. Have the children use a separate notebook page for each type of transition, allowing space to add to the list throughout the year.

— Note that students overuse the word *then* to show progressive action. *Then* we did this and *then* we did that. Model for the children how much more effective their writing is when the *thens* are omitted. I always ask permission to use a student's writing as an example, reading it first with all the *thens* in place and a second time without them. Then (whoops!) have the children examine their own work for places where they can line out unnecessary *thens*.

Beginning Lists of Transitional Words and Phrases:

time transitions: The next day. . . In a little while. . . Before long. . . Late in the afternoon. . . When it was time to leave. . . Before we knew it. . . The next thing I knew. . . When the bell rang. . . Later. . . It seemed like no time. . .

place transitions: Back in the kitchen. . . In the backyard. . . When we went upstairs. . .Out in the garage. . . In our classroom. . .

idea transitions: another reason. . . also. . . along with. . . one other thing. . . for example. . . would you believe. . .

summarizing: finally. . . for all these reasons. . . in conclusion. . .

You would not, of course, brainstorm all these types of transitions in one mini-lesson. Time and place transitions are more appropriately taught when children are working on personal narratives or fiction. Transitions from one idea to another and in summarizing are necessary in expository writing and should be introduced when children are working in that genre.

— The lists of transitional phrases in the children's notebooks will grow throughout the year as children come across them in their reading, in other children's writing, and as they use them in their own writing.

— Have the children examine a work-in-progress in their own folders to look for places where they used, or should have used, transitional words or phrases.

Mini-lesson 14
Write for Your Reader

Because the information is so clear in young writers' minds, they often forget that readers know only what writers tell them. In daily conversation, we often take shortcuts because we are able to use visual cues such as gestures and facial expressions that help convey our meaning. But in writing, words alone have to do the job. Teach the children to ask themselves the question, "What does the reader need to know?" as they read over their work. In time, they will begin to internalize the question and will keep the question in mind during their writing.

Non-example: Drip castles is dry sand and you get water and put wet sand then take some wet sand out and drip it on the dry sand and get it real tall and then you've got it!

(Sarah Smith, 3rd grade student, taken from *Write to Be Read*, Alleyside Press: 1992.)

Tell students that when Sarah wrote this description, the process was very clear in her mind—but not at all clear to a reader. After Sarah's conference group questioned her about the procedure for making drip castles, Sarah rewrote the description this way:

Example: *Make a pile of sand on the beach. Then go down to the ocean, and get water in a bucket. Now put sand in the bucket, not from the pile, but from the sand that is extra. Now take a handful of the wet sand and put it on the pile of sand. Get it tall, then you've got it!*

(Sarah's revision.)

See "Write for Your Reader—Sarah's Story," pages 112-113.

We were playing tether-ball at recess. While I waited for my turn, I talked with my friend, Susan. The next thing I knew, he smacked the ball so hard it came off the rope. Whack! It hit me on the side of my head.

We were playing tether-ball at recess. While I was waiting for my turn, and talking with my friend Susan, Jimmy stepped in to play. The next thing I knew, he smacked the ball so hard it came off the rope. Whack! The ball hit me on the side of my head.

Mom and I held hands tightly as we waited on the corner. Cars seemed to be rushing at us from every direction. Horns tooted. He blew his shrill whistle. People hurried by.

Mom and I held hands tightly as we waited on the corner of Fifth Avenue, the busiest street in New York City. Cars seemed to be rushing at us from every direction. Horns tooted. A policeman blew his shrill whistle. People hurried by.

Dad blew his stack when he got home. He took one look at it and started yelling, "I can't believe you did this again!"

Dad blew his stack when he got home. He took one look at my mangled bike and started yelling, "I can't believe you did this again!"

This is how you do it. You take one piece and spread it with peanut cover. Then cover it with jelly. Then put another piece on top. Enjoy.

This is how you make a peanut butter and jelly sandwich. First, spread one piece of bread with a layer of peanut butter. Then spread a layer of jelly over the peanut butter. Put another slice of bread on top of the first slice. Enjoy!

See "Write for Your Reader—Sarah's Story," pages 112-113.

As you share the non-examples, either by writing them on the chalk board, showing them on an overhead, or by reading them aloud, ask the children to identify the problem in each one. What information is missing? What questions are created in the mind of the reader? Why is the piece not clear? How would the children rewrite each passage? Having the children rewrite the passages for clarity in their notebooks and **sharing** their revisions is much more effective than showing them the rewrites in the examples.

Yes, yes, I know—**sharing** again! But, trust me—sharing is crucial to the success of your writing program.

The practice for this lesson is most productive if the children work together in pairs or triads, reading one another's work for clarity and asking questions when there is something that is not clear to the reader. Writers should then rewrite the confusing sections and have them read again to see if they are more clear.

Here's one way to organize a peer conference group.

I often divide the class into groups of three to five children. Each child is given a conference form on which they write their own names, the date, and the title (or topic) of their piece. They choose one member of the group to be the first secretary and one to be the first reader. As the reader reads his or her piece, the others in the group listen carefully and jot down any questions they may have. After the piece has been read, each person in the group has an opportunity to ask questions or make comments. The secretary records the questions/comments on the reader's conference form. After each member of the group has had an opportunity to contribute, a new secretary and a second reader is chosen. In this way, every child has an opportunity to read and be a secretary.

See "Peer Conference Form," page 97.

Quite often we evaluate an activity in writing workshop by discussing the children's perceptions—how they liked the activity, what worked and didn't work, and what we might do differently next time. The children tell me they enjoy this conferencing activity and especially appreciate having several other people respond to their work. I am constantly amazed at the quality and sophistication of their questions and comments. More often than not, the observations they make and questions they pose are very similar to ones I might have.

Resources

Christelow, Eileen. *What Do Authors Do?* New York: Clarion Books, 1995.

Schrecengost, Maity. *Write to Be Read.* *Wisconsin:* Alleyside Press, 1992.

Mini-lesson 15
Variety Adds Spice

For children who are learning to read longer and more complex sentences, writing long sentences seems better. We often see long, run-on sentences in their work. As children become fluent writers, they may become reluctant to use short pithy sentences. They need to be shown how alternating long and short sentences makes writing more interesting—and easier—to read.

Non-example: The cold wind blew through the leafless trees making me shiver.

Example: *The cold wind blew through the leafless trees. I shivered.*

My dog, Rusty, ran away and I felt very very sad.
My dog, Rusty, ran away. I cried.

Flames tore through the burning building and I heard the fire engine's siren blow.
Flames tore through the burning building. A siren screamed.

Kids pushed and shoved to be first in line, teachers were yelling, and it was chaos.

Kids were pushing and shoving to be first in line and teachers were yelling. It was chaos.

The first time we saw the Grand Canyon, it was so beautiful it took our breath away and we couldn't say a word.
The first time we saw the Grand Canyon, its beauty took our breath away. We were speechless.

Having children count the number of words in sentences in their own writing is a good strategy. If they see their sentences are nearly all the same length, it becomes a challenge to rewrite them for variation. Counting the number of words also helps children recognize run-on sentences.

Resources

Bunting, Eve. *Nasty Stinky Sneakers*. New York: HarperCollins Publishers, 1994.

Stein, R. Conrad. *The Story of the Flight at Kitty Hawk*. Chicago: Children's Press, 1981.

> **TIP**
>
> *Reading children's work out loud helps them to hear the rhythmic flow and to become aware of how a shorter sentence breaks the cadence, adding interest to the sound patterns. Having someone else read their work is more effective than reading it themselves. When writers read their own work aloud, they often read what they **meant** to say, or what they **thought** they said, rather than what they actually wrote.*

Mini-lesson 16
S-t-r-e-t-c-h a Sentence

Just as children need to learn to vary sentence length by using an occasional short pithy sentence, they also need practice in learning to expand sentences. This mini-lesson encourages sentence expansion by adding descriptive and/or specific details.

Non-example:　　The old man walked slowly.
Example:　　*The tired old man limped unsteadily, tapping his cane in front of him.*

A boy played in his yard.
A five-year-old boy played with his dump truck in the back yard sand box.

The kitten played with string.
The fluffy white kitten swiped at the string with its tiny paw, lost its balance, and tumbled over on its back.

Dad is working in the garage.
Dad drilled holes in the piece of wood and then sanded them smooth by hand.

Grandma fixed the car.
Grandma lifted the hood and said, "Just what I thought. A loose connection on the carburetor!"

Extending the Lesson

— Write the words *who, what, how, where, when, why,* and *result* vertically on the chalkboard. Invite one child to write a naming noun beside *who*. He chooses another child to write an action beside *what*. The next child chosen writes to tell *how* the action took place. Continue in this fashion until all the information is in place. The result might look something like this:

who	lady
what	planted seeds
how	carefully
where	in the soil
when	early one morning
why	she loved flowers
result	she had a pretty garden

Good writers often expand their sentences.

A short sentences:
The man walked slowly.

Example
The tiered old man limped unsteadily, tapping his cane in front of him.
　　　　　　　　　　　　^ wooden

Practice
A fifteen-year old boy play with his golden retriever Goldy in his one acre yard.

Practice
The black spatted dalmation barked loudly in the back yard of the neighbors house.

— Invite the children to add descriptors by asking questions like: What else do you know about the lady? (she's sweet, gray-haired, old, etc.) What kind of seeds did she plant? (pansy, sunflower, etc.) How deep did she plant them? (depends on the seed!) Where was the soil? (in her front yard, back yard). Record their answers on the chart.

— Now have the children incorporate as much of the information as they can in only one sentence. This will be a real challenge for them and you will want to give lots of help! The results may look something like this: Early one morning, a gray-haired lady planted pansy seeds in the soil in her front yard because she loved flowers and wanted to have a pretty garden.

— The children should examine their own works-in-progress for places where sentences could be stretched and made more interesting by adding more information.

See "Ask Yourself These Questions As You Write," page 101.

Resources

Heller, Ruth. *Many Luscious Lollipops: A Book About Adjectives.* New York: Grosset and Dunlap, 1989.

Heller, Ruth. *Up, Up and Away: A Book About Adverbs.* New York: Grosset and Dunlap, 1991.

Roderman, Winifred Ho. *Writing 1: Getting Started.* CA: Fearon/Janus,1990.

TIP

As you continue to conference your students, asking questions to elicit more information and helping them to "take another look" at their work, they will begin to internalize the questions you pose. Then they are ready to begin to self-conference, asking questions that will help refine their work.

Mini-lesson 17
Crunch Sentences

Children who are accustomed to writing short, choppy sentences need practice combining sentences to tie several ideas together. Lessons in grammar books often teach sentence combining using the conjunctions *and, or*, and *but*. This mini-lesson demonstrates combining ideas without overusing conjunctions.

Non-example: I was happy. The sun was shining. It was the first day of summer vacation.

Example: *I was happy that sunny first day of summer vacation.*

Andrew felt sick. His head ached. His stomach hurt.
Andrew's aching head and hurting stomach told him he was getting sick.

It was noisy. Dogs were barking. Radios blared. My ears hurt.
The noise of barking dogs and blaring radios hurt my ears.

I love Colorado. I like the huge mountains. Colorado has sparkling streams.
I love Colorado's huge mountains and sparkling streams.

It was so dark. I heard strange sounds. I felt scared.
Strange sounds in the darkness scared me.

Divide class into triads or pairs. Give each group three short sentences. At a given signal, the groups compete to see which group can compose a "crunched" sentence first. Encourage the children to avoid overusing conjunctions. Share the sentences from each group and repeat the activity using new sets of three short sentences.

Resource

Roderman, Winifred Ho. *Writing 1: Getting Started*. CA: Fearon, Janus, 1990.

TIP

A spirit of playfulness should be evident in writing labs. Show delight in the children's efforts, rejoice with them in their successes, and "pick them up, dust them off, and set them on their feet again" when something doesn't work the way they planned. Let the children in on your own writing successes—and failings—as you work together in an exciting, risk-taking, exploratory environment.

Mini-lesson 18
Bring Your Characters to Life

When we think about people we know, we think of them in terms of what we know about them: their likes and dislikes, their quirks and foibles. Children generally identify characters in their writing by name only. We need to help them see that names are labels that may or may not give information about the character. Just as people do in real life, each character in a piece of writing should have a unique personality and display identifying characteristics.

Non-example: Joey is a kid in my class.
Example: *Joey scratched the mosquito bite on his knee through the hole in his pants.*

    Ms. Green, my teacher, came into the room.
    Ms. Green's purple skirt swirled and her red hair bounced as she entered the room.

    Butch, the school bully, was on the playground.
    With a sneer on his face, Butch swaggered across the playground.

    Priscilla is the cleanest kid in our class.
    Priscilla dusted her seat with her hanky and smoothed the skirt of her dress before she sat down.

    Ralph is smart and always gets good grades.
    Ralph pushed his glasses up on his nose and smiled knowingly when the teacher handed out the three page test.

TIP

Of course, ground rules for what is acceptable in the descriptions are essential!

With this mini-lesson, I often have each child choose a person in the classroom. Without telling who they have chosen, each writes a character sketch of their chosen person. They may not use names or describe the clothing their person is wearing and they must include one identifying characteristic of the person's personality. The children take turns reading their sketches aloud while the rest of the class tries to identify the character from the description.

Resources

Dahl, Roald. *Danny The Champion of the World*. New York: Puffin Books, 1988.

Dahl, Roald. *Matilda*. New York: Viking Press, 1988.

Lindgren, Astrid. *Pippi Longstocking*. New York: Puffin Books, 1997.

Parish, Peggy. *Amelia Bedelia*. New York:HarperCollins Juvenile Books, 1992.

Mini-lessons 19 through 23
Give Your Characters Personality

As children discover favorite characters in the books they read, they find they like the characters, not only because of how they look, but because of the things they do, and say, and think. Learning to make their characters come alive by the way they look and the things they say, do, and think is an advanced skill, but kids can do it! And they are so proud when they do!

Mini-Lesson 19 - Characters look different. . .

Non-example: Sally stared at me.
Example: *Sally tossed her blonde pony tail and stared at me through her wire rimmed glasses.*

Mrs. King spoke to our class.
Mrs. King stood with one hand on her hip and scowled before she began speaking in a stern voice.

Janie is worried.
Janie's brow wrinkled in a frown.

I knew Petey was up to something.
Petey's eyes twinkled and he wore a mischievous grin.

Alice was scared half to death.
Alice's face turned white as a sheet and her eyes nearly bulged out of her head.

Mini-Lesson 20 - Characters act differently. . .

Non-example: Tommy is sad.
Example: *Tears filled Tommy's eyes as he bit his lip to keep from crying.*

Mom was upset.
Mom threw the dish towel down on the counter before she sent me to my room.

The little old lady was confused.
The little old lady put her eye glasses in the refrigerator and the salad by the television.

He was a kind boy.
He looked down at the small boy and bent to help him pick up the dropped books and scattered papers.

That was one pesky raccoon.
Every night the curious raccoon pried the lid off our garbage can and spread its contents across our lawn.

My little sister is a real brat.
My little sister comes into my room when I'm not there, reads my diary, and plays dress-up with my favorite outfits.

Mini-lesson 21 - Characters speak differently. . .

Non-example: Laura's feelings were hurt.
Example: *"I can't believe you did that to me," said Laura, in a trembling voice.*

Jackie is frustrated.
"I never do anything right," moaned Jackie.

Julie is lonely.
"If only there was one other girl my age in this neighborhood," wailed Julie.

Sonny is afraid that he'll do badly on the math test.
"Oh, boy, oh, boy," moaned Sonny, "one more bad grade in math and I'm off the softball team."

Heather thinks she's hot stuff.
"Naturally," said Heather, "I'll be elected class president. I mean, I'm the obvious choice!"

Mini-lesson 22 - Characters think differently. . .

Non-example: Kathy hates math.
Example: *"I wish I never had to see another math problem as long as I live," thought Kathy.*

Jackie feels sick.
"My head hurts and I feel like I'm going to throw up," Jackie thought miserably.

Joanie feels misunderstood.
"Why doesn't anyone around here understand anything," wondered Joanie.

Gretchen is frustrated.
" I must be the dumbest kid in the class," stewed Gretchen. \

Mom wishes the rest of the family would help around the house.
"Apparently I'm the only one in this house who knows how to wash dishes," fumed Mom.

Only one attribute will be taught in a session, of course. Allow plenty of time for the children to practice rewriting the non-examples. After lessons 19-22 have been introduced and practiced, let the children write sentences demonstrating one of the attributes. As the sentences are read aloud, the listeners should be able to identify the character trait that is demonstrated in the sentence.

Mini-lesson 23 - Put them all together. . .

Non-example: Judy was angry when Mrs. Grinch assigned fifty problems for homework.

Example: *Judy scowled, wrinkling her sun-burned nose, as she said, "I can't believe that old meany gave us fifty problems!"*

Jolene was sad when her best friend moved away.
Jolene swung slowly back and forth on the swing as she wiped away tears with the back of her hand. "I'll never have a friend like Kelly again as long as I live," she thought.

Chip hated losing the last game of the season.
Chip stuffed his ball cap in his pocket and kicked at a clod of dirt as he stomped back to the dugout. "The last game," he thought, "why did we have to lose the very last game?"

Jessie was excited about going to California.
"No way!" Jessie screeched. "Are you serious? I mean, are we really going to California?" she asked, jumping up and down like a happy frog.

Ms. Dilly had a bad headache.
Please, children," Ms. Dilly pleaded while pressing her temples with both hands, "I can't stand another sound!"

After modeling, but before teaching the extensions for practice, use the example and non-example and engage in a pre-writing activity. Asking the children to think about what they do, say, or think when they are sad, frustrated, excited, or ill will help the children "get inside the skin" of the characters in the scene.

Resources

MacLachlan, Patricia. *Sarah Plain and Tall*. New York: Harper & Row Publishers, 1985.

O'Dell, Scott. *The Black Pearl*. New York: Dell Publishing, 1967.

Schrecengost, Maity. *Write to Be Read*, Chapter 9. Wisconsin: Alleyside Press, 1992.

Wojciechowska, Maia. *Shadow of a Bull*. New York: Atheneum, 1974.

TIP

Have fun with creative dramatics with this one! Act out one of the personality traits for the children to identify. Then let the children take turns acting them out. The kids love this activity, and it provides lots of visual clues and language for them to use in their descriptions and dialogue.

Mini-lesson 24
What's in a Name?

Children very often name the characters in their stories for their best friends. In this mini-lesson, they have great fun seeing how a character's name is often a clue to the character's personality and that choosing good names for their characters is important.

Brainstorm favorite characters in literature and discuss why the authors chose those particular names. Examples that come to mind are Wilbur, in E.B. White's *Charlotte's Web,* Pippi Longstocking, and Willy Wonka. Why did A. A. Milne name the tiger Tigger in *Winnie-the-Pooh*?

Non Example: Christopher, the class bully, stalked across the play ground.

Example: *Max, the class bully. . .*
                Butch, the class bully. . . etc.

The principal, Mr. Fish, stepped up to the microphone.
The principal, Mr. Learn, stepped up to the microphone.

My favorite teacher, Miss Hornwhistle, entered the classroom.
My favorite teacher, Miss Honey, entered the classroom.
(from Roald Dahl's *Matilda)*

Our family dentist, Dr. Greenspan, said, "Sit down and make yourself comfortable."
Our family dentist, Dr. Drill, said, "Sit down and make yourself comfortable."

Our history teacher, Mr. Black, adjusted his spectacles.
Our history teacher, Mr. Century, adjusted his spectacles.

TIP

Remind the children that characters are never all good or all bad. Even the worst villain has some redeeming trait and no one wants to read about a character who's perfectly perfect all the time!

Extending the Lesson

— Cut out pictures of a variety of people: kids, grownups, cartoon type drawings. Have the children suggest names for the characters that seem to fit the way the characters look. Then have the children tell something a character with the given name and appearance might do.

— Working together, choose two, or at the most, three, of the characters and weave them into a class story. As you record the story on chart paper, remind the children that the character's name should provide clues to the character's dialogue and action.

Resources

Greenwald, Sheila. *Here's Hermione. A Rosy Cole Production.* Boston: Little, Brown and Company, 1991.

Havill, Juanita. *It Always Happens to Leona.* New York: Crown Publishers, 1989

Mini-lesson 25
Try Tags

Characters in the stories children write are often homogeneous. It's hard to tell one from another. Tags are devices writers use to identify a character when he or she appears in the story. Tags may be gestures, characteristic mannerisms, habits or personality quirks. Posture or manner of speech may be used as tags.

By recognizing character tags and practicing using them students give their characters unique identities.

Non-example: Susie was thinking hard.
Example: *Susie tugged at her ear lobe as she thought about the question.* (From now on, when the writer wants to show that Susie is thinking, he can simply have her tug on her earlobe.)

Ms. Dreyfus was getting annoyed.
We kids knew Ms. Dreyfus was getting mad when she flared her nostrils.

Millie was really excited.
Millie walked with that funny little half skip step she takes when she's excited.

My little sister, Julie, is getting tired.
Mom knew Julie was tired when she began digging at her eyes with both fists.

Extending the Lesson

— Encourage the children to think about each of their classmates and try to identify tags—characteristic mannerisms—for as many as possible. Have them write a paragraph involving two class members including a characteristic tag for each one. Allow the children to share their paragraphs while classmates try to identify the class members described.

— Encourage the children to incorporate a tag or two into one of their narrative works-in-progress.

Resource

Peck, Robert Newton. *Soup.* New York: Knopf Edition, 1998.

TIP

Kids usually want to include all their friends in their stories. Remind them to not overpopulate their stories. Have them try limiting the characters to two or three. Encourage them to make their stories more real by including characters with different types of personalities.

Mini-lessons 26 through 31
Be Sensible!

Although children are very aware of the sensory world, they aren't skilled at using words to appeal to the reader's senses. They want to say, "I see. . ." or "I hear. . . " It takes many examples of teacher modeling and plenty of opportunities for children to practice using sensory words instead of *telling* the reader what is seen, heard, smelled, tasted, or felt.

Mini-lesson 26 - Let the reader see what you see. . .

Non-example: I saw a beautiful sky.
Example: *Shades of orange, blue, lavender, and gold spilled across the late afternoon sky.*

We came upon a desert .
Cactus reached their arms to the cloudless blue sky.

It was a clear night.
The moon floated in the star studded sky.

A jet flew overhead.
Like a silver bullet in the sky, the jet left a white trail.

Resource

O'Neill, Catherine. *You Won't Believe Your Eyes*. Washington, DC: National Geographic, 1987.

Mini-lesson 27 - Smell what you. . .

Non-example: Woods have their own special smell.
Example: *The musty odor of moldy leaves, the fragrance of pine needles, and the smell of rich dark earth fills the woods.*

A circus has lots of smells.
The fragrance of straw and popcorn mingled with the stench of elephant dung.

Dad was cutting grass.
The perfume of gasoline and new mown grass drifted around the corner of the house.

Nothing smells like a locker room.
Smelly sneakers, disinfectant, sweat— you've gotta love a locker room!

We're having pizza for dinner.
Oregano, tangy tomato sauce, and spicy pepperoni told my nose we were having pizza for dinner!

Resource

Moncure, Jane Belk. *What Your Nose Knows*. Chicago: Children's Press, 1982.

Mini-lesson 28 - Hear what you. . .

Non-example: It was a loud parade.
Example: *Trumpets blared, the bass drum boomed, and children shouted as the parade came down our street.*

I heard kids on the playground at recess.
The crack of a bat hitting the ball, kids yelling, and the sharp blast of a teacher's whistle echoed across the playground.

The school cafeteria is noisy.
The cafeteria echoed with the sounds of silverware clattering, trays banging, and kids chattering happily as they ate.

The orchestra is tuning up.
Clanging cymbals, screeching violin strings, high piercing piccolo notes, and the tapping of the conductor's baton let us know the concert would soon begin.

There must have been an accident.
Screeching tires and the crash of metal followed by a siren's wail could only mean an accident.

Resource

Moncure, Jane Belk. *Sounds All Around*. Chicago: Children's Press, 1982

Mini-lesson 29 - Taste what you. . .

Non-Example: Lemonade tasted good on such a hot day.
Example: *The icy cold lemonade left a tartness in my dry mouth.*

I love the taste of popcorn.
Salt mingled with the buttery flavor of the hot white kernels.

Pizza is my favorite food.
Spicy pepperoni, Italian herbs, tangy tomato sauce on a thick browned crust. What more could I want?

Liver and onions, how disgusting!
Slimy slivers of onion coiled on top of a wet brown slab. I felt myself begin to gag.

Who can resist peanut butter and jelly?
Yum! The rich nutty flavor mingled with the grape jelly and the whole beautiful glob stuck wonderfully to the roof of my mouth.

Mini-lesson 30 - Feel what you. . .

Non-example: We walked along the beach.
Example: *Broken shells on the hot sand hurt our feet.*

I love to walk in mud.
Cold wet mud oozed between my toes.

I hate it when my sister eats crackers in bed.
I rolled over. My sister's cracker crumbs crunched against my bare skin. I hate that!

Ouch — I have a blister on my heel.
My sock was sticking to my skin and my heel stung like mad bees were attacking.

Nothing beats the feel of running through a sprinkler on a hot day.
Nothing beats the sensation of cool droplets of sprinkler water sizzling on my hot skin.

Resource

Otto, Carolyn. *I Can Tell by Touching*. New York: HarperCollins Publishers, 1994.

Mini-lesson 31 - . . . .and now. . . put them all together. . .

Non-Example: A circus is exciting.
Example: *The blare of cornets and the booming bass drum announced the start of the circus. Splintery bleachers scratched my legs. Colorful pennants flapped high above the ring. The buttery smell of popcorn mingled with the musty odor of animals and straw.*

It's a perfect day at the beach.
Fluffy white clouds float in the brilliant blue sky. I drop my bold striped beach towel on the hot sand. Broken shells hurt my feet as I race for the water. Sea gulls scream overhead. I plunge into the water, licking salty sea spray from my lips, but soon the smell of hamburgers sizzling on the grill lures me back to shore.

Breakfast is ready.
Coffee perking, sizzling bacon, butter melting on perfectly browned pancakes, and a growl in my stomach let me know that breakfast is ready.

We broke a window playing ball.
Crack! Crash—the sound of splintering glass. I tasted fear as I pictured Dad's face when he saw the window.

Spelunking is a different experience.

When we crawled into the cold, damp cave my skin felt clammy. Dad's flashlight pierced the blackness. Water dripped from the top of the cave, ghostly white above our heads, forming stalactites. Bat guano covering the floor of the cave made my breakfast rise to the occasion. Did I really want to do this?

Extending the Lesson

You might teach each sensory mini-lesson by itself, or do two or three senses within one lesson. The time available and the children's interest are the determining factors.

Resource

McMillan, Bruce. *Sense Surprise: A Guessing Game for the Five Senses.* New York: Scholastic, 1994.

TIP

Encourage children to explore sensory images both in the classroom and outdoors. I often take the children outside with paper, pencil, and clipboards to sit quietly and list everything they see, hear, smell, and can feel. Later, they use their lists to write descriptions of "The World Outside My Classroom."

My World

In my world I can hear the wonderful sound of nature: birds chirping, mosquitos buzzing, and much, much more.

In my world I can smell the flowers that have just bloomed and the freshly cut grass.

In my world I can see beautyful birds soaring high in the sky above. I can see the beauty of nature.

In my world I can feel the tiny bugs that crawl on my skin. I can feel the cool breeze that blows in my hair.

It is the world I live in, and it is the world that is mine and only mine.

By Sarah Schmitt

Sarah attempts to explore the senses in this piece.

Mini-lesson 32
Mood Magic

Children learn to recognize that some stories make them laugh or feel happy, others make them sad, and still others may be scary. The emotional tone of the story is its mood. Setting the mood lets the reader know how he should expect to feel as he reads. When children have learned to identify mood in stories they have read, they're ready to learn how authors use words to create moods. They will enjoy learning to create some moods of their own. Help the children identify mood words like the ones in bold type in the examples.

Non-example: It was a scary night.
Example: *Clouds drifted across the moon, trees* **cast shadows** *on the* **deserted** *road, and an owl* **hooted** *from a tree limb overhead.*

Aunt Alice felt peaceful on the hillside. (peaceful)
Aunt Alice lay on her back watching **clouds form smoky pictures** *in the sky while a* **meadow lark sang** *sweetly nearby.*

Being alone in the dark house was spooky. (mysterious)
I was all **alone** *in the* **dark** *house when I heard* **heavy foot steps** *on the porch. Slowly the door* **creaked** *open. I heard a soft* **thump**.

The sound signaled danger. (danger)
Suddenly the hair on the **back of my neck** *stood up. I heard a* **rustle** *in the brush nearby followed by a* **hiss** *and an* **ominous** *rattling sound.*

It was fun being with grandpa. (humor)
"Well **jumpin' jodhpurs**," *said Gramps, holding up the now* **two foot tall Christmas tree.** *"I do b'leve I cut off* **a mite too much!"**

Extending the Lesson

— A colleague, Nancy Byers, suggests playing classical music to help children understand the concept of mood. As the children listen, encourage them to talk about how the music makes them feel. Play the music again and, this time, have the children write about what they imagine is happening as they listen. The results are often amazing!

— Explore the concept of mood by asking students what mood they might experience in a church or synagogue (awe, reverence, peace), at a theme park or video arcade (excitement), in a hospital? At school? At their birthday party?

TIP

Children may have a difficult time understanding mood. It helps them grasp the concept if you tell them a mood of danger should make the reader say, "Uh, oh!"; a peaceful mood makes the reader say, "Ahhhh"; a scary mood, "Oooooh," and a humorous mood will make the reader grin. It's great fun when they read their practices aloud and the class responds with the appropriate sounds or facial expressions.

For each, brainstorm words and/or phrases that might be used to convey the identified mood to a reader.

Have the students select a setting and write a paragraph or two to create the appropriate mood.

— Let students who wish to share their work read their passages aloud to the class with appropriate background music.

Resources

Beethoven, Ludwig Van. *Ode to Joy.*

Handel, George Frederick. *Water Music.*

Haydn, Joseph. *Surprise Symphony.*

Saint-Saens, Camille. *Carnival of the Animals.*

Tchaikovsky, Peter Ilyich. *The Nutcracker Suite.*

Fleischman, Paul. *Rondo in C.* New York: Harper & Row, 1988.

Sommer, Elyse. *The Kids' World Almanac of Music from Rock to Bach.* New York: Pharos Books, 1991.

Mini-lessons 33 through 37
Show Your Character's Feelings

Just as authors use words to create mood (the emotional tone of a piece), they also use words to convey the feelings the mood generates. Writing to show feelings is especially fun for children this age. Encourage the children to recognize feeling words noted in the examples in bold print.

Mini-lesson 33 - Love

Non-example: Betsy loves her kitten.
Example: *Betsy **cuddled** her kitten and **rubbed her cheek** against its soft fur.*

Joey loves his grandpa.
*Joey **snuggled** on Grandpa's lap and sighed **contentedly**.*

Lucy loves chocolate ice cream.
*Lucy licked the chocolate ring **framing her wide smile**.*

Sammy loves his dad.
*Sammy's **eyes shone** as he **gazed** at his dad with **admiration**.*

Our teacher loves reading to us.
*Ms. Jones **smiled** as she **settled comfortably** into her rocker before carefully opening the chapter book she'd been reading to us.*

Mini-lesson 34 - Anger

Non-example: Mom was really angry.
Example: *Mom's eyes **blazed** and her **voice shook** when she **shouted**, "Go to your room this minute, young man!"*

I was angry when I saw Butch tormenting the kitten.
*I felt like **grabbing Butch around the neck** to **shake the daylights** out of him when I saw him tormenting the kitten.*

Ms. Ellis seemed angry.
*Ms. Ellis's **nostrils flared** and her **voice quivered** when she said, "Class, this behavior is **unacceptable!"***

Fido was angry when we put him on his leash.
*Fido, **barking wildly, strained against the leash** and **pawed** the ground.*

The blue jay was angry when the mockingbird invaded its territory.
*The blue jay **flew restlessly** from branch to branch, **squawking raucously** at the **unwelcome** invader.*

Mini-lesson 35 - Frustration

Non-example: Jimmy was upset that he wasn't allowed to go, too.
Example: *Jimmy **clenched and unclenched** his **fists** as he argued, **"But, Mom,** everyone else in the whole class is going."*

Jerry wasn't able to solve the math problem.
*Jerry **bit his lip, frowned** at the math paper, and began **tapping his pencil impatiently** on the desk.*

Dad was irritated that he couldn't stop the faucet from leaking.
*Dad **threw the wrench aside** in **disgust** saying, **"I give up;** I'll **have to call** a plumber!"*

The writer was annoyed by the incessant ringing of the telephone.
*When the phone rang again, the writer **jumped up, stomped** over to the phone, and **yanked the phone jack** out of the wall.*

Mom couldn't get the thread through the small hole in the needle.
*After **trying several times** to thread the needle, Mom **stabbed it** into the pin cushion and **muttered, "Well, who cares?** I didn't want to sew that button on **in the first place."***

Mini-lesson 36 - Loneliness

Non-example: Alice felt so all alone.
Example: *Alice **pressed her nose** against the window pane, **watching** the kids playing in the park across the street.*

Janie hated going into the house alone.
*Janie took the **key from around her neck** and unlocked the door, knowing **no sound would greet her** from the **empty rooms.***

Being the new kid is a lonely experience.
*The new kid stood **nervously** at the door of the classroom **filled with happy chattering kids** and felt like she was **invisible.***

It was the first time Jimmy had stayed alone when his parents went out.
*When the door **closed behind Jimmy's parents,** the rooms of the house seemed strangely bigger, **filled with vast empty space.***

Julie felt sad as she watched her dad's plane take off.
*As Julie watched the huge jet **carry her dad to far off places,** she felt a **great hole begin to form** inside her chest.*

Mini-lesson 37 - Happiness

Non-example: Chris was so happy.
Example: *Chris's face broke into a **wide grin** as he jumped up and down, shouting, "**All right!**"*

Melody woke feeling happy.
*Melody woke with a **smile** on her face and a **tingle of happy excitement** in her tummy.*

Our dog was happy to see us again.
*When we picked Rusty up from the vet's, he **raced around in circles, yipping happily**, and **licking each of us** in turn.*

The kids were happy the last day of school.
*The kids **burst through the doors, shouting merrily**, "No more teachers, no more books; No more teacher's dirty looks!"*

Our test grades made the teacher happy.
*"**Wow!**" our teacher exclaimed. "These fantastic grades call for a **celebration!**"*

Extending the Lesson

— In pairs or in small conference groups have the children examine one another's work-in-progress. Ask the conference partners to find and circle words or phrases that show feelings. You may prefer to have them mark the passage(s) with a smiley face or comment. Then ask them to mark with a check or an X places where the writer could have shown feelings.

Resources

Aliki. *Feelings.* New York: Greenwillow Books, 1984.

Arnos, Janine. A series of books on feelings: *Hurt, Jealous, Lonely, Sad, Afraid.* US: Steck-Vaughn Company, 1991.

TIP

From time to time, post a picture or art print that shows strong feelings and invite the children to write about their impressions. Doing this early in the year and then having the children respond to the same work of art at the end of the year provides a wonderful tool to assess their growth as writers. Children can also write about art and post their work in the school hallways. What a wonderful way to make the writing and fine arts connection!

Mini-lesson 38
New-P, New-P Rule

Early on, children often write long unbroken narratives because they don't know how to clump their sentences into paragraph units. I'm including paragraphing as a mini-lesson because it is such an important organizing skill. A Pennsylvania colleague, Robert North, originated this wonderful way to teach paragraphing narratives. Robert calls it the New-P New-P Rule.

New-P, New-P Rule

New P-erson, New P-aragraph

New P-lace, New P-aragraph

New P-eriod of Time, New P-aragraph

New P-lot Event, New P-aragraph

New P-oint of View, New P-aragraph

Paragraph Power

Non-example: Mom's voice rang out from the kitchen, "Hurry up, Chip, you'll be late for school. I pulled on my jeans with the grass stain on the knee from the day I slid into home, then dug my dirty sweat shirt out of the laundry basket. It had a big chocolate splotch on the front and was pretty wrinkled. Then I dropped my lucky marble in my pocket. I was ready. When I went into the kitchen, my stomach lurched. Mom was cooking oatmeal. I hate oatmeal! Five minutes later, after I had covered the oatmeal with brown sugar and drowned the whole mess in milk, I was able to swallow it down without gagging too much. Then I bolted out the door before Mom could yell at me for wearing dirty clothes to school. Joey was already at the bus stop. He can be a real pain. He's also my best friend. His silly grin made me feel a lot better. But not for long. "Hey, Chip," he said, "where's your backpack?"

Example: *Mom's voice rang out from the kitchen, "Hurry up, Chip, you'll be late for school." I pulled on my jeans with the grass stain on the knee from the day I slid into home, then dug my dirty sweat shirt out of the laundry basket. It had a big choco-late splotch on the front and was pretty wrinkled. Then I dropped my lucky marble in my pocket. I was ready.*

When I went into the kitchen, my stomach lurched. Mom was cooking oatmeal. I hate oatmeal! But after I had covered the oatmeal with brown sugar and drowned the whole mess in milk, I was able to swallow it down without gagging too much.

Then I bolted out the door before Mom could yell at me for wearing dirty clothes to school.

Joey was already at the bus stop. He can be a real pain. He's also my best friend. His silly grin made me feel a lot better. But not for long.

"Hey, Chip," he said, "where's your backpack?"

See "Paragraph Power—Chip's Story," page 114.

This lesson is best taught by displaying the non-example on the board or overhead and helping the children recognize that it is hard to read because there are no paragraphs. Then display the New-P New-P Rule and show the children how it works.

Explain that using paragraphs is a powerful tool that breaks writing into readable units. After the children understand how to determine when to make a new paragraph, based on the New-P, New-P Rule, work with them to mark (ⁿ) where each new paragraph should begin. After that, show the correct example. I find it works well to read the piece aloud slowly and have the children clap softly whenever I reach a place in the text where a new paragraph should begin. Be sure to remind the children that the first section of any new piece of writing will be indented.

Show kids how to use planning strategies at the pre-writing stage. Lists, story boards, webs, time lines, story maps, semantic maps, outlines, and other graphic organizers help kids organize their ideas before they begin drafting.

Pieces lacking an organizational plan are difficult, if not impossible, to paragraph. Novice writers who are not yet able to organize their ideas cannot be expected to paragraph a jumble of ideas and/or impressions.

The **New-P, New-P** rule, with slight modifications, works for expository writing, too. The New P-lot Event would change to New P-oint. In other words, each new point the writer wants to make should have its own paragraph with topic sentence and supporting details. A final New-P for expository writing might be P-ull It All Together, a paragraph for summarizing the points made in the piece. The New-P, New-P rule for expository writing looks like this:

New-P, New-P Rule for Expository Writing

New P-iece, New P-aragraph

New P-oint, New P-aragraph

New P-erson, New P-aragraph

New P-lace, New P-aragraph

New P-eriod of Time, New-Paragraph

Now P-ull It All Together, New Paragraph

See "The New-P, New-P Rule," page 100.

TIP

Call children's attention to the use of paragraphs in their reading and content-area texts. Guide them in learning to recognize the reasons for making new paragraphs by applying the New-P, New-P rules.

The following piece, *My Favorite Way to Travel*, can be used to demonstrate paragraphing in expository writing:

(new piece)   Cars! Trains! Planes! Even cruise ships! There are lots of ways to travel. But if I had my choice, I'd choose planes every time.

(new period of time)   Last year I flew for the very first time to Kansas to visit my grandparents. I had a blast and knew then that flying would forever be my favorite way to travel. It was so much fun, I didn't want the plane to land even though I was glad to see my grandma and grandpa.

(new point)   Flying is fast and, for someone like me who is impatient, that's important. The last time we went to Kansas, we went by car. I thought we'd never get there! It took five whole days of driving, driving, driving. By plane the whole trip only took three hours. I didn't have time to get restless.

(new person)   Of course, my Mom said I should have enjoyed the scenery from the windows of the car. But I said, "How many wheat fields can one person enjoy seeing?"

(new point)   Speaking of seeing, that's another thing great about flying. I loved looking out the window at the midget cars and doll houses far below us. Rivers looked like brown ribbons and swimming pools seemed to be the size of postage stamps. The world looks totally different from way up in the sky.

(new point)   Another neat thing about flying is that the stewardesses bring food to you. There's a cute little tray that pulls down from the back of the seat in front of you to use while you're eating. I'm not saying it's the best food in the world, but it sure beats starving to death while you wait for your Dad to decide to stop for gas or a lunch break! On the flight to Kansas, we had little turkey sandwiches, individual bags of chips, applesauce, a chocolate chip cookie, and fruit juice.

(new place)   When we landed in Kansas City the airport was a beehive of activity. Flying is exciting because there's so much to see and do at the airport. People rushing to catch their flights, planes coming in and going out, and announcements over the loud speakers made my head spin!

(pull it all together)   Yes, the speed of flights, the fun of observing the world from on high, the novelty of eating airline food from little trays, and the excitement of airports all convince me that flying is the only way to go!

See "Paragraph Power—Flying is the Way to Go," page 115.

TIP

Sometimes the text goes on and on and none of the New-P, New-Ps seem to apply. In that case suggest to the children that they make a new paragraph at a logical point just to break up the text to make it easier on the reader's eyes.

The following non-example and example can be used to demonstrate breaking text at a logical point.

Non-example: The first step when you are doing a research report is to choose the topic. Not only is this the first step, it may well be the most important one. Choosing your topic well can make the difference between a finished report that is interesting to read and one that is only ho-hum. Choose a topic that is interesting to you. If you are not interested in the subject, it will be very hard to write a report that is enjoyable for others to read.

Example: *The first step when you are doing a research report is to choose the topic. Not only is this the first step, it may well be the most important one. Choosing your topic well can make the difference between a finished report that is interesting to read and one that is only ho-hum.*

Choose a topic that is interesting to you. If you are not interested in the subject, it will be very hard to write a report that is enjoyable for others to read.

From: (*Research to Write*. Alleyside Press: 1994)

See "Paragraph Power—Logical Breaks," page 116.

Have the children look at their own work-in-progress and mark the text where paragraphs should be. Having the children work in pairs to check each other's work is a good technique as they learn to apply the New-P, New-P Rule.

Mini-lesson 39
Weed That Garden!

Beginning writers tend to overuse words like *so, then, and*, and *so then.* They feel they need to connect their ideas or introduce new thoughts by using these words as bridges. It has been my experience that children are so accustomed to using these words that they don't recognize they aren't very useful until it is pointed out to them. I like to make the analogy that these words are like weeds in a garden; they add nothing and detract from the beauty.

TIP

Students love to write on overhead transparencies. Call on a child to come up and line out a "weed." Then let the student call on a classmate to find and line out another.

Adding variety to the lesson format increases involvement and heightens interest.

Non-Example: It was chilly that last day in March. So I put on my jacket and headed for school. And on the way I saw some thing sparkling in the grass beside the road. So I picked it up. And it was a diamond! Then I looked all around to see if anyone was looking for it. And no one was. So then I didn't know quite what to do. Then I dropped the diamond into my shirt pocket. And then I went on to school.

Example: *It was chilly that last day in March. I put on my jacket and headed for school. On the way, I saw something sparkling in the grass beside the road. I picked it up. It was a diamond! I looked all around to see if anyone was looking for it. No one was. I didn't know quite what to do. I dropped the diamond into my shirt pocket. Then I went on to school.*

See "Weed That Garden," page 117.

Write this paragraph on the board or on an overhead, then ask one of the children to read it aloud or read it aloud yourself. Then ask students to tell you what is wrong with the piece.

You may be confounded by their answers! My kids said things like, "Well, how did he know it was a diamond?" and "The kid's dumb! Why would he go to school after he found a diamond?!" One said, "How could he look all around? His head wouldn't turn that far!" (Moments like this sometimes cause me to question my career choice—to say nothing of my sanity!) I had to read the piece a second time, emphasizing the "weed words" in order for them to hear the problem.

Point out that words like *and, so, so then*, etc. aren't workers. They don't *do* anything in the sentence and they clutter things up. They're like weeds in a garden and must be pulled out to make the garden (writing) more lovely (graceful.) Together, go back over the paragraph and line out or delete all the "weeds." Then have the new version read aloud so the children can hear how much more smoothly the writing flows.

You'll find that this lesson needs to be repeated. I always ask permission to read aloud a student's piece of writing that has lots of weeds. I read it first with all the "weeds" and then again without them. Children do not easily pick this up by reading silently because readers, both children and adults, often overlook these words. We tend to let our eyes slip over them, and they go unnoticed. Children recognize "weed words" more easily when they hear them read aloud.

Extending the Lesson

— Follow up this lesson by assigning students to examine one of their own "works-in-progress" or finished works to locate and eliminate "weed" words.

Mini-lesson 40
Support Your Great Ideas

TIP

This is such an important reading and writing skill. You will want to return to this mini-lesson many times throughout the school year. It cannot be repeated too often.

Still being somewhat egocentric, students at this age think nothing of making a statement or giving an opinion without giving information to back it up. Their philosophy is, *It is because I said so!* (Honesty compels me to admit that this is sometimes my philosophy, too!)

Intermediate-age children are learning to recognize supporting details in their reading texts and are encouraged to use supporting details from the text when writing short-answer essay questions. This mini-lesson gives students practice in using details to support their ideas as they write them down.

Non-example: I think it's going to rain.
Examples: *The sky is dark and I hear thunder. I think it's going to rain.*

It's a gorgeous day.
The sun is shining and the sky is crystal blue.

No one cares about me.
I've been crying for an hour, my eyes are all red, and all anyone can think about is my brother's ball game.

Jimmy is a great ball player.
Not only is Jimmy a good pitcher, he nearly always gets a hit when he's up to bat.

The manatee is a trusting creature.
The gentle manatee shows little fear of humans and may approach them with curiosity.

When you present each non-example, pose a question. For the non-example, "It's a gorgeous day," ask, "What makes a day gorgeous? What do you think of when you hear the words *gorgeous day*? " For the non-example "No one cares about me," ask, "Why would the writer feel that way? Have you ever felt like that? What made you feel that no one cared about you?" Help the children look for the unanswered question behind every unsupported statement.

This lesson makes a good reading-writing connection. As the children learn to recognize how writers "back-up" or "prove" what they say in texts they read, they will begin to use details in their own

Last night when I was stuck on my math, good old Dad showed me how to solve the problem. Yep - my dad is one-in-a-million!

My mom is a terrific cook!

Kelly is my real true friend. Kelly ceps secerets when I tell her to. She plays with me when she promises to. She helps me with my work sometimes. When I don't feel good, she is there to comfort me. I can trust her. She is my true friend.

Helping students explore the unanswered questions behind unsupported statements ensourages detail-rich writing.

writing to support their ideas. This mini-lesson also helps kids prepare for performance-based reading tests in which they must support their answers with details from the passage read.

Resources

Buckley, Helen E. *Moonlight Kite*. New York: Lothrop, Lee & Shepard Books, 1997.

Lamar, William W. *The World's Most Spectacular Reptiles & Amphibians*. Tampa: World Publications, 1997.

Mini-lesson 41
Examples Give Extra Support

Examples are another kind of higher level supporting detail that children need to learn to use. While details give additional information to support, or "hold up," the statement, examples provide additional support with little stories or personal anecdotes, quotes from famous people or authorities, information drawn from reading, researched information, or statistics that prove or support the point being made.

Non-example: Tyler School is the best school in the county.
Example: *Tyler is the best school in the county. Once our teachers took us on an overnight camping trip.*

My dad is the greatest!
My dad always has time to listen to me and help me. Last week I was really stuck on my math and Dad showed me an easier way to solve the problem. personal anecdote

Summer is my favorite season.
Last summer I went to the beach almost every day. statistical information

This is the worst day of my life!
Even my best friend, Joey, said, "I can't believe what a rotten day you've had!" quote

Day Geckos vary in both size and color.
Day Geckos may be a few inches or nearly a foot long and they may be brilliant green, blue, yellow, red, orange or tan. researched information

Teach this mini-lesson by challenging the children to find examples to prove each non-example. For "My dad is the greatest!", ask kids to suggest personal anecdotes or little stories that show a great dad. Challenges like: "Show me!" or "Prove it!" or "How can you tell? What information do you have?" stir the kids to create convincing examples that support their ideas.

Here's an acronym that helps children remember to use supporting details and examples. T.E.S.S. works like this:

T-ell your idea.
E-xplain the idea.
S-upport the idea with a detail.
S-upport the idea with an example.

Of course, you can add on more S's for more details and examples! For a main idea paragraph in a piece about choosing a favorite place to visit, T.E.S.S. might look like this:

T - I'd love to visit Australia to see the unusual animals that live there.

E - Australia has all kinds of animals that don't live in the United States. Because Australia is an island, animals there are different from ones found other places. I'd love to see them in their native habitat.

S - I'd give anything to see kangaroos in the outback, wombats burrowing long tunnels at night, koala bears feeding in a eucalyptus tree, or the emu, a bird that can't fly.

S - Animals in Australia sure are different. My friend, Jim, says that in Australia, kangaroos are road kill! And he ought to know because he lives there.

See "T.E.S.S.," page 118.

Resources

Betz, Adrienne. *Scholastic Treasury of Quotations for Children*. New York: Scholastic, 1998.

Bitton-Jackson, Livia. *I Have Lived a Thousand Years, Growing Up in the Holocaust*. New York:Scholastic, Inc., 1997.

Freedman, Russell. *Indian Chiefs*. New York: Scholastic Inc., 1987.

Senn, J. A. *Quotations for Kids*. Connecticut: The Millbrook Press, 1999.

TIP

T.E.S.S. works well with graphic organizers. Show students how to use the T.E.S.S. for each main point.

Mini-lesson 42
Get Real!

Because writing seems more "formal" than speaking, young writers may write stilted dialogue. Once they learn how much fun it is to write the way people really talk—including dialects and jargon!—their writing begins to take on a distinctive flavor.

Non-example: "Hello," said Sally, "please come into my house."
Example: *"Hi," said Sally, "come on in!"*

"That's not how we do it in England," said Reginald.
"I say, old chap," said Reginald, "that's really not the way we do it in England."

"Give me that ball, or I'll take it from you," said Butch.
"Gimme that ball, twerp, or you'll be sorry," snarled Butch.

"If you say another word, Billy, I may find it necessary to give you an in-school suspension," said the principal.
"One more word, young man, and it's an in-school suspension for you!" snapped the principal.

Extending the Lesson

Have the children practice writing dialogues of three or four sentences involving two distinctly different characters: a scholar and a bully; themselves and their mom; a student and a principal, or perhaps a city kid and a country kid. You might bring in creative dramatics by having several children role play the parts while the others write down, or tape record to transcribe later, what they hear the actors say.

Introduce children to the difference between dialect and jargon. *Dialect* is a form of language peculiar to a locality or group that differs from standard or formal speech. *Jargon* refers to the special vocabulary and idioms of a particular group or class of people. For example, we might think of Southern dialect, clipped Yankee speech, or Black dialect, as opposed to the jargon of circus folk, sports teams, teenagers, teachers, or educational jargon.

So often we fail to take advantage of the cultural diversity in our schools. Call attention to the richness and beauty of the native languages of your ESOL students. Encourage kids to listen for similarities and differences. This is also a wonderful opportunity to teach word derivation, English words derived from other languages.

> "Hey" said Pa, "are you ready yet? The wagon be leaven' in a short time now." "Alright I'm acomin I'm acomin." So we loaded onto the wagon. We were movin' west to Texas. As we were riddin' Sal and Chandler were playin' marbles while Pa was drivin' the wagon and Ma was weaving.

The use of dialect brings life to dialogue.

Resources

Avi. *What Do Fish Have to Do with Anything?* Mass: Candlewick Press, 1997.

Dahl, Roald. *James and the Giant Peach.* (British). New York: Alfred A. Knopf, 1961.

Harris, Joel Chandler. *Uncle Remus Tales. His Songs and Sayings (New Revised Edition).* New York: Grosset and Dunlap.

Lenski, Lois. *Strawberry Girl.* (Cracker) New York: Dell Publishing, 1945, 1973.

TIP

Be sure to read aloud from books that contain various dialects. Kids love the sounds of language and are eager to try their hands at writing realistic dialogue.

Mini-lessons 43 and 44
Sensational Similes

Children are learning to recognize similes and metaphors in their reading. *Similes* are figures of speech in which one thing is likened to another dissimilar thing using the words like or as. An example would be the phrase, *The sun is like a giant beach ball*. A *metaphor* is a figure of speech containing an implied comparison. In a metaphor a word or phrase ordinarily used of one thing is applied to another. For example: *a sheet of rain* or *a curtain of fog*. Mini-lessons such as the next two help students learn to use metaphorical language.

Mini-lesson 43 - Sensational Similes

Non-example: The road curved.
Example: *The road curved like a brown ribbon through fields of wheat.*

The water sparkles in the sunlight.
Sunlight sparkles on the water like diamonds.

The angry man roared.
The angry man roared like a wounded lion. (Kids always say "roared like a wounded lion," but, hey, we all have to start somewhere!)

Her hair is all tangled.
Her hair looks like a bird's nest.

The Amazonian Horned Frog has horns sticking out of the top of its head.
The Amazonian Horned Frog looks like a green devil with horns sticking out of the top of its head.

Mini-lesson 44 - Magnificent Metaphors

Non-example: The sun is shining high above us.
Example: *The sun is a blazing fireball high above us.*

The palm trees sway in the breeze.
The palm trees are Hawaiian dancers.

The stars are bright.
The stars are sparkling diamonds.

The river twists through the canyon.
The river is a watery snake slithering through the canyon.

The sheepswool sponge is very valuable.
The sheepswool sponge is Gulf Coast gold.

TIP

Using similes and metaphors in their writing is not a daily event for young writers. Reward them by setting aside a special spot in your room for Notable Quotes. When kids use a simile or metaphor, or write an especially powerful sentence, have them write the sentence on a colorful sentence strip and post it in your Notable Quotes Corner.

Use any—or all—of the resources listed to read aloud similes and metaphors. *You Dance Like an Ostrich* is especially good. The first half of the book is similes, and the second half metaphors, both presented in a very humorous style with terrific illustrations.

Resources

Hanson, Joan. *Similes: As Gentle As A Lamb, Spin Like a Top.* Joan Hanson Word Books. (Hard to find—try Harvest Booksearch.)

Juster, Norman. *As Silly as Knees, As Busy as Bees. An Astounding Assortment of Similes.* New York: Morrow Junior Books, 1998.

Juster, Norman. *A Surfeit of Similes.* New York: Morrow Junior Books, 1989.

Tester, Sylvia Root. *You Dance Like an Ostrich.* 1978. (Hard to Find. Filled by Harvest Booksearch. This one is worth searching for.)

TIP

Encourage the children to be alert to similes and metaphors in reading texts and recreational reading.

Mini-lesson 45
Say What?

Children, and adults for that matter, tend to use words in both speech and writing that don't really say anything. I call them "non-words." The non-words that I'm referring to are not just slang words, which do have meaning for the "in group" using them. Non-words, to me, are words that don't convey much meaning.

Some of my kid's favorite non-words in writing are *stuff, cool, weird, lots of things, and much more, nice, good. . .* I'm sure you get my point.

Young writers need to be reminded to say exactly what they mean and not assume the reader will understand their "non-words." For example, a lunch that I think is quite "good," may to them be "nasty." Words carry different connotations to different people. Choosing specific, descriptive words instead of non-words allows the reader to know what the writer actually means.

Non-Example: Our teacher is cool.
Example: *Our teacher lets us do our math outside under the trees on sunny days.*

Chuck is so weird.
Chuck never wants to do what other kids do, and he reads the dictionary!

We did a lot of fun stuff on my birthday.
We had dinner at Pizza Hut and then went to see Toy Story on my birthday.

Florida has interesting birds, like the egret and much more.
Florida has interesting birds, like the egret, the flamingo, the ibis, the wood stork, the anhinga, and the pelican, to name only a few.

This book is so dumb!
This book has no plot and the characters are totally unbelievable.

Following the mini-lesson, the children should look at their own work to find examples of non-words and revise them to say exactly what they mean.

Mini-lesson 46
Get Noisy with Onomatopoeia

Children love to write words in capital letters for emphasis. Onomatopoeia, the use of words that imitate sounds associated with the action or object, is often written in all capitals, providing a perfect opportunity for kids to do what they do naturally anyway! They do need to be cautioned to not overdo it, but, at first, let developing writers explore sound words and have a ball with them.

Non-example: The door opened with a loud noise.
Example: *The door opened with a BANG!*

The balloon burst.
POP went the balloon!

It's really cold.
BRRRRR. It's cold.

We heard the train whistle.
The train whistle echoed, TOOT TOOT.

My little sister screamed at the sight of the mouse.
"EEEK! " my little sister screamed at the sight of the mouse.

The sound of the ticking clock drove me nuts.
The TICK TOCK, TICK TOCK of the clock drove me nuts.

Encourage the children to keep an ongoing list of onomatopoetic words in their notebooks. They enjoy grouping the words as animal sounds, people sounds, and thing sounds.

Resources

DeZutter, Hank. *Who Says a Dog Goes Bow-Wow?* New York: Stewart, Tabor and Chang, 1993.

Robinson, Marc. *Cock-a-Doodle-Doo!* New York: Doubleday Books for Young Readers, 1993.

TIP

Kids enjoy working together in pairs to create simple fun stories with lots of onomatopoeia to share with younger children in lower grades. This activity gives purpose for writing and provides opportunities for sharing.

Mini-lesson 47
Alluring Alliteration

Alliteration, the repetition of a sound at the beginning or end of side-by-side or nearby words, is another literary device. Writers use alliteration to create a pleasing sound in the reader's inner ear as he reads. Children are familiar with alliteration in tongue twisters, like Peter Piper picked a peck of pickled peppers, and in rhyming poetry, such as "Roses are red, Violets are blue; Sugar is sweet, And so are you." They are less apt to notice alliteration as it appears in prose. Children get excited when they begin to recognize the pleasant effect of alliteration in the books they read, and even more excited when they are able to use it in their own writing.

This lesson heightens children's awareness of alliteration and is fun for them to practice. The appearance of alliteration for effect in student writing will probably be serendipitous. When you do notice alliteration in a student's work, invite the writer to share it with the class.

TIP

Alliteration may be created by repeating starting consonants, end consonants, consonant blends, or whole first syllables of words.

| Non-example: | It is a huge tree. |
| *Example:* | *It is a tree of tremendous size.* |

We stepped into a snow covered forest.
We stepped into a winter wonderland.

What a gloomy day!
What a gray day!

The sled runs fast down the snowy hill.
The sled flies pell mell down the slippery slope.

> Stuborn Sam said "this stinky sausage is spoiled
> Tina told the teacher that I tickled her toes.
>
> Stuborn Sam said, "This stinky sausage
> is spoiled."
>
> Tina told the teacher that I tickled her toes.

Practice with alliteration is fun and heightens awareness of this important writer's technique.

Resources

Kellogg, Steven. *Aster Aardvark's Alphabet Adventures.* New York: William Morrow and Company, Inc., 1987.

Heller, Nicholas. *Goblins in Green.* New York: Greenwillow Books, 1995.

Mini-lesson 48
Don't Keep the Reader
in the Dark!

Foreshadowing is a literary device that intermediate-age children are beginning to become familiar with. In foreshadowing the author hints or indicates that a certain thing might, could, or will happen later on in the story. In other words, the writer gives the reader clues. Authors use foreshadowing to heighten reader's interest, to move a story along, and to help give the story continuity.

This is a sophisticated skill. You shouldn't expect many intermediate-age students to be able to incorporate it into their own writing. For the sake of those one or two talented writers in your classroom who may be able to use it, and for the benefit of all who will become aware of the technique, it's worth introducing.

As you read aloud to students, stop when you come to an example of foreshadowing. Ask the children to predict what they think might happen later on in the story. Ask them to be specific when telling the clues that led to their predictions. Later, help them recognize when their predictions were correct — or incorrect! Encourage students to identify examples of foreshadowing in the books they read on their own.

Example: Chapter 5 of my book, *Panther Girl*, ends with an example of foreshadowing:

> *Mariah wondered often that day as she petted wounded Rascal and waited for Daddie's return, if she, like Mam said, would ever have to "just do" something—and if she would really be brave enough to do it.*

When the children in my classroom read the ending to this chapter, their eyes grew big and they "just knew" that later on Mariah would be faced with a scary challenge. They were eager to read on to find out what the scary challenge would be. When, toward the end of the book, they came to Mariah's decision to enter the swamp to warn her Seminole friends, several children called out, "That's it!"

Extending the Lesson

— The best extension for this mini-lesson is ongoing. Use foreshadowing as an opportunity to explore "author's intent" by engaging the children in discussions of why an author might use foreshadowing. Talk about how foreshadowing helps the reader.

— Encourage children to give the reader hints of what is coming in their own writing.

TIP

Foreshadowing occurs in daily life when. . .

. . . .dark clouds roll in

. . . .the is unusually dressed up

. . . .Mom goes on a cleaning frenzy

All are hints of something to come, and examples of the kinds of foreshadowing students can use when they write.

Challenge the children by presenting them with story situations in which foreshadowing would be useful. For example, how might they foreshadow getting a new puppy? (Perhaps dreaming about a puppy early in the piece or gazing at a puppy in a pet store window)

How could they foreshadow the main character's loss of an expensive ring? (a parent's warning early in the story to be careful with the ring)

. . . .a cross country trip?
. . . .parents' divorce?
. . . .a new baby in the family?

— Encourage students to examine a narrative-in-progress to see if foreshadowing could be used.

Resources

Avi. *The True Confessions of Charlotte Doyle*. New York: Orchard Books, 1990.

Fleischman, Paul. *The Half-a-Moon Inn*. New York: Scholastic Inc., 1980. (This is one of my all time favorites. Don't miss it!)

O'Dell, Scott. *The Black Pearl*. New York: Dell Publishing, 1967.

Mini-lesson 49
Keep 'em in Suspense!

Cliff-hangers are another literary device that intermediate-age children are becoming familiar with. A cliff-hanger is the device of ending a chapter with a question—usually implied—that compels the reader to read on. Most children this age are not writing chapter stories, but they should learn to recognize cliff-hangers when they occur in stories they read. And there may be a talented student in your class who wants to try this literary device.

It's important to introduce literary devices like foreshadowing and cliff-hangers to developing writers, even though not many of them will be able to successfully use the devices in their writing. Introducing such literary devices makes developing writers aware of author's intent. Beginning writers write to write. Developing writers begin to write with more purpose. Advancing writers will begin to write with intent and will ask themselves questions about choices they make.

Example: *Jonas' heart swelled with gratitude and pride. But at the same time he was filled with fear. He did not know what his selection meant. He did not know what he was to become. Or what would become of him.*

From *The Giver,* by Lois Lowry.

This cliff-hanger ends Chapter 8 of Lois Lowry's *The Giver.* It surely makes the reader want to read on. Roald Dahl is a master at writing cliff-hangers. Nearly every chapter in *James and the Giant Peach* ends with one. Like this one at the end of Chapter 35 when the giant peach went hurtling toward earth:

"Help!" cried the Centipede.

"Save us!" cried Miss Spider.

"We are lost!" cried the Ladybug.

"This is the end!" cried the Old-Green-Grasshopper.

"James!" cried the Earthworm. "Do something, James! Quickly, do something!"

"I can't!" cried James. "I'm sorry! Good-bye! Shut your eyes everybody! It won't be long now!"

From *James and the Giant Peach* by Roald Dahl.

Extending the Lesson

— This mini-lesson is also an ongoing one as children watch for cliff-hangers in the books they read and/or during read aloud times. Be sure to call attention to cliff-hangers when you read aloud to children. A tantalizing cliff-hanger should result in children crying, "Oh, no! Don't stop now!" My kids accused me of always stopping with a cliff-hanger when I read to them—and, of course, they're right. I did!

— Use cliff-hangers as opportunities to talk about author's intent. Engage the children in discussions about why authors use cliff-hangers and how they are useful to an author. Discuss, too, how cliff-hangers may help readers.

Encourage students to keep records of cliff-hangers in their reading logs.

Resources

Banks, Lynne Reid. *Indian in the Cupboard*. New York: Avon Books, 1980.

Bulla, Clyde Robert. *A Lion to Guard Us*. New York: Harper Trophy Reissue Edition, 1989.

Dahl, Roald. *Charlie and the Great Glass Elevator*. New York: Alfred A. Knopf, Inc., 1972.

Pierce, Tamora. *Alanna: The First Adventure*. New York: Random House, 1989.

Mini-lesson 50
Use a Little Hype!

Children are familiar with hyperbole, the use of exaggeration for effect, if for no other reason than that they hear us use it so often, as in: "I've told you ten thousand times, 'Don't sharpen crayons in the pencil sharpener!'" Kids use hyperbole naturally in their speech: "I have tons of homework." "A bazillion flies covered the picnic table."

Exaggeration is fun, and children love learning to use hyperbole in their writing. Of course, their first attempts may be quite outlandish! But, then, that's part of the fun!

Non-Example: It was really cold.
Example: *It was so cold, tears formed icicles on my eyelashes.*

Mom made a lot of mashed potatoes.
Mom made a mountain of mashed potatoes.

Jerome is a fast runner.
Jerome can outrun a cheetah!

Our teacher gives us too much work
Our teacher gives us tons of work every day.

The jar was filled with marbles.
There must have been sixty million marbles in that jar!

Extending the Lesson

— This is a fabulous time to work with Tall Tales—the ultimate example of exaggeration. Encourage the children to write their own larger-than-life tales and perhaps publish an illustrated class collection of their stories.

Resources

Osborne, Mary Pope. *American Tall Tales.* New York: Alfred A Knopf, 1991.

San Souci, Robert D. *Larger than Life. The Adventures of American Legendary Heroes.* New York: Doubleday Books for Young Readers, 1991.

TIP

Remind children that there's a difference between a "plain old lie" and hyperbole! Hyperbole is used for effect, to make a point, and isn't meant to be taken literally!

Mini-lesson 51
Say It With Meaning!

Children love to use all capital letters for emphasis, as when they use onomatopoeia. They instinctively know that some words need to be emphasized. But all capital letters may be too explosive when the writer wants to merely stress the word. In print, these words are usually in italics. Even young writers can learn the judicious use of an occasional underlined word for emphasis.

Non-example: No, she is not my friend.
Example: *No, she is <u>not</u> my friend.*

                     You mean he ate the whole thing?
                     You mean he ate the <u>whole</u> thing?

                     So when did they come to America?
                     So when <u>did</u> they come to America?

                     I absolutely love hot fudge sundaes.
                     I absolutely <u>love</u> hot fudge sundaes.

                     That is the silliest thing I've ever heard.
                     That is the <u>silliest</u> thing I've ever heard.

Extending the Lesson

— Have students examine their own work to find a few words that might be underlined for emphasis. Let them share their findings so others can hear the difference when the sentences are read with selected words emphasized and without emphasis.

— Tape record a class discussion at a time when the children aren't aware you are doing so. (Be sure to choose a time when the discussion is likely to be lively!) Type the conversation and make an overhead transparency. During a writing workshop, show the transparency and play the tape recording asking the children to identify which words they hear might be italicized if the conversation appeared in a book.

Resource

Dahl, Roald. *Charlie and the Chocolate Factory.* New York: Alfred Knopf, 1985.

TIP

This mini-lesson makes a listening connection. Students this age are writing speeches and engaging in public speaking. Exercises like this one develop an awareness of the importance of word choice, the connections between written and spoken language, and the importance of voice inflection. Remind students that readers hear the writer's words in their heads.

Mini-lesson 52
An Anthropomorphic Angle!

Although children may not be familiar with the word *anthropomorphism,* they've encountered this literary device in their reading from the time they were very small. Many of their favorite stories are striking examples of anthropomorphism, the attribution of human characteristics to animals or things. Chicken Little, the toys in *The Velveteen Rabbit,* Peter Rabbit, and the little engine in *The Little Engine that Could* are familiar examples.

Gather a collection of fables, folk tales, and other books like the ones mentioned above that are good samplings of the anthropomorphic genre. As you share these with the children, point out that the human characteristics attributed to the characters must be in keeping with what they know about the animal or inanimate object. For example, the timidity of Chicken Little is appropriate for our ideas of a hen, but would hardly work if she was a hawk or rooster. Similarly, Peter Rabbit's antics wouldn't have been believable had Beatrix Potter made him Billy Beaver.

Extending the Lesson

— Encourage students to think of ways in which animals and/or things are similar to people. Brainstorm with the class lists of a variety of animals and/or inanimate objects and characteristics that might be appropriate for each and inappropriate for others. For example: **dog:** brave, loyal, wise; **horse:** strong, intelligent; **fox:** sly, sneaky; **rooster:** braggart, noisy, proud; **beaver:** industrious, busy; **frog:** impetuous, silly, big mouth. Or **a little engine:** hard working, determined; **teddy bear,** affectionate, loving, loyal; **puppet,** mischievous, curious. Have students keep these lists in their notebooks so that they can add to them as they encounter examples of human characteristics attributed to animals and things in their reading.

This lesson is a good one for group story writing. I suggest this because of a personal experience. My class entertained a visiting author. As part of her presentation, she involved the children in writing a group story. First, she asked them to choose a setting. They chose the beach. She encouraged them to not choose their friends for the characters, but to choose characters that were different. (A good idea.) But, they chose a fox, a fish, and a chicken! Then, when she asked them to come up with a problem, they decided the problem was that the fox, the fish, and the chicken were lost on the beach and couldn't find their way home.

Can you imagine the confusion that ensued! Our visiting author handled the situation very well, but . . . Working through writing a group story teaches children that even in fantasy stories where animals talk, the setting, situation, and problem have to be believable and have a reasonable solution.

After you have worked through the process of writing a story in this genre together, try the next extension.

— Invite the children to write their own fables involving several animals in which they can practice ascribing human characteristics to the animals.

— Once the children have enjoyed ascribing appropriate human characteristics to animal characters, it can be even more fun to write a story in which the animal displays unlikely characteristics. Play the "What if . . ." game. What if the beaver was lazy? What if the hawk was nearsighted? What kind of story would result if the rooster was too timid to crow?

Resources

Harris, Joel Chandler. *Complete Tales of Uncle Remus*. New York:Houghton Mifflin Co., 1955.

Lawson, Robert. *Rabbit Hill*. New York: Puffin Books, 1944, 1972.

Leaf, Murro, *The Story of Ferdinand*. New York: Viking Press, 1987. (Although this is for younger readers, it's a good read-aloud example of a character exhibiting traits that are the opposite of what one would expect).

Lobel, Arnold. *Fables*. New York: Harper & Row Publishers, 1980.

O'Brien, Robert. *Mrs. Frisby and the Rats of NIMH*. New York: Atheneum, 1974.

Silverstein, Shel. *The Giving Tree*. New York: HarperCollins Juvenile Books, 1986.

TIP

Combine anthropomorphism with alliteration by encouraging the children to use both in stories to be read to children in lower grades.

Mini-lesson 53
Bring Things to Life

Personification is a figure of speech in which a thing is represented as a person, or in which a person or thing represents a quality or idea. For example, children know that Cupid represents (is the personification of) love and a four-leaf clover stands for good luck. The use of a person or thing to represent qualities or ideas is too abstract for younger children to be able to incorporate into their writing, but they can grasp the idea of things having human attributes. Upper level intermediate writers will be able to do so.

Non-example: Wind blew through the trees.
Example: *The wind whistled through the trees.*

A boulder blocked our path into the woods.
Like a mighty sentinel, a boulder guarded the path.

The sun felt warm.
The sun smiled on us.

Water bubbled in the stream.
Bubbling water sang a merry song.

The raccoon was in our garbage can again.
The little pirate raided our garbage can again.

Help students make this abstract connection by asking one child to name an inanimate object. A volunteer then supplies a word that names something a living thing does or is that could apply to the inanimate object. Some examples: couch-groans; leaves-dance; brook-sings; sun-smiles; road-beckons; bed-invites; pasture-sleeps; snow-blankets; fence-guards; tree-waves, and so on. This lesson can turn into a rollicking good time!

> **TIP**
>
> *This exercise provides a wonderful opportunity to encourage kids to "think outside the box." Encourage risk-taking by reminding the kids that there are no wrong answers!*

Resources

L'Engle, Madeleine. *A Wrinkle in Time.* New York: Yearling Books, (Reissue) 1997.

Lewis, C. S. *The Lion, the Witch, and the Wardrobe.* New York: Macmillan Publishing Company, 1950.

Young, Ed. *Lon PoPo.* New York: Philomel Books, 1989.

Mini-lesson 54
Try a Rhyme

Children and rhyme go together. From early finger plays, to rhyming books, to jumping rope chants, children learn to rhyme. Most children think rhyme, not rhythm, is the basis of poetry. Many of their rhyming experiences have to do with end rhymes; sounds that reappear at the end of lines. They may not be so aware of how rhyming words side-by-side or interspersed within the sentence can help the text flow more smoothly and add to the imagery in the text.

Non-Example:	It's a good time to play.
Example:	*It's a fine day to play.*

The sunlight woke us up.
We woke to the bright light of morning.

One lone star twinkled in the sky.
One lone star twinkled afar.

The hawk flew in circles in the dusty sky.
The hawk made lazy circles in the hazy sky.

Early on, student attempts at writing poetry, or using rhyming words within prose, are forced and often don't seem to "fit." Help children recognize that rhyming words not only have similar sounds, but have some sort of relationship.

This exercise, similar to the one in Mini-lesson 53, stretches the mind and is fun, too.

Choose a word and write it on the chalkboard. Tell students they are to think of a word that rhymes with the word on the board and be able to tell how the two words are related. For example, if you wrote the word *sky,* some related rhyming words might be *high* (for obvious reasons!); *fly* (birds fly in the sky); *cry* (the sky looks like it's crying when it rains), etc. *Dye* or *fry* on the other hand are not good rhymes because there seems to be little relationship between them and *sky.*

Other rhyming possibilities might be *moon*-balloon (looks like) and June (love 'n stuff); *stream*-dream (a place for dreaming); *sleep*-deep (sound asleep); weep- (if you're having a bad dream.) You can expect a lot of creative thinking with this exercise—it will probably produce some unexpected responses!

Resources

Larrick, Nancy. *When the Dark Comes Dancing: A Bedtime Poetry Book.* New York: Philomel Books, 1983. (Wonderful poetry that doesn't rely on end rhymes.)

Yolen, Jane, Editor. *Street Rhymes Around the World.* Honesdale, PA: Wordsong Boyd's Mill Press, 1992.

Mini-lesson 55
Surprise Your Reader!

Who doesn't like surprises? And kids love them most of all! When I read aloud to children, one of the things they enjoy best is a surprise twist in the story. Helping kids learn to put surprises in their stories is fun for them and for you. Sometimes their surprises may be a bit too much to be believable, but then, that's a lesson for another day!

Teach this lesson by reading passages from literature with good examples of plot twists, or surprises.

In *Panther Girl*, Mariah, the heroine, is trying desperately to be brave as she makes her way through the darkening swamp.

Clutching her panther claw, Mariah moved on. A rat snake slithered across the path in front of her. Mariah clenched her teeth. A cold chill ran over her body. A few steps more. Splat! Something cold and wet landed on her cheek. Brushing it off frantically, the thing plopped in front of her. A tree frog! It was nothing but a tree frog.

From: *Panther Girl*. Maupin House, 1999.

See "Panther Girl," page 119.

Help kids stretch their imaginations to look beyond the obvious. Tease their gray matter by asking *What ifs*. . . "What if Goldilocks had still been in the cottage when the three bears came home?" "What if Snow White had said, "No, thanks. I don't care much for princes." "What if the giant peach hadn't been impaled on the spire of the Empire State Building?" "What if your dad came home on your birthday, threw open the door, and shouted, 'Sorry, kid! No birthday present this year!'" "What if you put your tooth under your pillow and the "tooth fairy" left a plane ticket to South America?"

See "Panther Girl," page 119.

Extending the Lesson

— Ask the children to think of (or imagine) a situation in their own life when there was an unexpected turn of events. Suggest they write about it.

Resource

Dahl, Roald. *Danny, The Champion of the World*. New York: Puffin Books, 1975.

TIP

Remind children that a surprise does not have to shocking. A well-planned surprise is an unexpected turn of events or an incident within the plot that has an unusual twist.

Mini-lesson 56
Could You Repeat That?

People who repeat themselves in conversation are soon known as bores. But in writing, repetition can be an effective literary device. Children are familiar with repetition in some of their old favorites: Chicken LIttle's "The sky is falling," the pattern in *This is the house that Jack built,* and the Little Engine's "I think I can, I think I can. . . " Some of their earliest writing attempts may have been extensions of pattern books where they wrote their own versions of *Someday. . .* or *The Very Best Thing About. . .* They are less apt to realize that writers (including themselves) may use repetition for emphasis or for special effect.

Non-example: The frogs croaked all night long.
Example: *All night long we listened to the frogs' croaking, croaking, croaking.*

Mariah and Daddie's walking seemed endless.
Mariah and Daddie walked. And walked. . . and walked.

The rain continued for days.
For days it rained and rained and rained.

Kristos and I will work hard to pay back what we owe.
Kristos and I will work hard—hard, I tell you—to pay back what we owe.

No, you can't borrow my sweater.
No. Absolutely not. I will never let you borrow my sweater.

TIP

This is it—your final reminder. Don't neglect the sharing time!

Discuss and list some times a writer might use repetition. For example:

- to show ongoing action
- to show action that seems to go on forever
- to emphasize a point
- to emphasize a quality
- to emphasize a negative
- to show excitement or joy

Extending the Lesson

— Take students to the media center to find examples of repetition. Tell them they are to copy each example that they find and beside it write the author's intent in using repetition. Not only will the children find examples of repetition and explore author's intent, they will look at a variety of trade books. And, they will get out of the classroom for a brief time which will bring them great joy! Be sure to remind them to look at poetry books and examples of expository writing.

Resource

Aardema, Verna. *Why Mosquitoes Buzz in People's Ears.* New York: Dial Press, 1975.

Mini-lesson 57
Color Your Dialogue
with Colloquialisms

Children love the feel of new words on their lips. Learning big grown-up words like colloquialism, meaning a phrase that is characteristic of informal speech, is a real treat. Colloquialisms are idioms, conversational phrases, and informal speech patterns, often common to a particular region or nationality. Not found everywhere, colloquialisms are the words, pronounciations, and phrases that we learn at home rather than at school. Help the children recognize that colloquialisms are not sub-standard or illiterate speech.

Colloquialisms vary from one part of the country to another, forming part of our oral, rather than our written, culture, and that reflect both its diversity and the richness. Encourage children to use colloquialisms common to your region in their personal narratives. Have them examine a personal narrative or fiction piece in their folders to see if they have used, or could insert, a colloquialism in the dialogue to sharpen a character.

TIP

This is a great vehicle for developing listening skills. It also helps children become more aware of the differences between poor grammar and informal speech.

Non-Example: I have to straighten up my room before I can play.
Example: *I have to redd up my room before I can play.* (Eng. or Scot. origin)

Please pass the bread.
Pass me down over the table the bread. (PA Dutch)

There's no more paper.
The paper is all. (South central PA, probably PA Dutch origin)

Don't you know?
Don'cha know? (Informal)

That's not going to work.
That dog won't hunt. (Texas)

It's a fine day.
It's a wonderful gut day. (Amish)

I hope you will all come.
Y'all come now, ya hear. (Southern)

Ouch!
Oofdah! (Minnesota)

Didn't anyone ever teach you anything?
H'ain't cha got no fetchin' up? (rural Ohio)

Who are that baby's parents?
Who's that baby for? (southern Louisiana)

Extending the Lesson

— Children have great fun finding colloquialisms in the books they are reading and listening for them in daily conversations. Make a class collection. Research the origins of the colloquialisms to include with the collection.

Resources

Cassidy, Frederic G., Chief Ed. *Dictionary of American Regional English.* MA: Harvard University Press, 1985

(Be sure to check out the web page: http://polyglot.lss.wisc.edu/dare. Newsletters are available and the web site has a quiz page. Fun!)

http://www.rootsweb. com/~genepool/sayings.htm

Ye Olde English Saying. This is another fun site at which you can search the meanings of common English sayings. You can subscribe to a discussion group and/or send questions about the origins of common English phrases at: words-l@rootsweb.com. **Caution: This site is not for students!**

Mini-lesson 58
Season Your Dialogue with Idioms!

Children enjoy learning to recognize, interpret, and use idioms, which refers to the language or dialect of a people, or the usual ways in which words of a particular language are joined together to express an idea. Children are more familiar with idioms as phrases that have a meaning other than the literal meaning. Idioms add flavor and color to writing when used sparingly.

Idioms can give rise to hilarious illustrations. Build a wall of idioms in your classroom. Have the children illustrate the idioms showing the literal and interpretive meaning of each.

Non-Example: I tried to get her to look at me.
Example: *I tried to catch her eye.*

That guy really irritates me.
That guy really gets my goat.

I was so mad.
I saw red!

Hubert is so annoying.
Hubert is such a pain in the neck.

I can't put up with this anymore.
That's the last straw!

Resources

Cox, James A. *Put Your Foot in Your Mouth.* New York: Random House, 1980.

Terban, Marvin. *Mad As a Wet Hen.* New York: Clarion Books, 1987.

Terban, Marvin. *Punching the Clock.* New York: Clarion Books, 1990.

Terban, Marvin. *Scholastic Dictionary of Idioms.* New York: Scholastic, 1998.

TIP

Kids do tend to be quite literal. Quite often when I read aloud to them, a figure of speech or pun that I think is supremely funny sails right over their heads. Be sure the kids "get" the intended meanings of the idioms.

Mini-lesson 59
Lively Allusions

Very few young writers will have the sophistication to use literary allusion in their own writing, but they can learn to recognize it in the literature they read. Literary allusion, where the author alludes to another well-known piece of literature by using a phrase or passage from it, adds richness to the text. A few of your gifted or talented writers may begin to use this literary device.

Non-Example:	It looks like we're headed for trouble.
Example:	*We're not in Kansas anymore, Toto!*
	We've reached our destination.
	We've reached the Promised Land!
	Sally's afraid of everything.
	Sally's always sure the sky is falling.
	I'm so confused!
	I feel like Alice in Wonderland!
	I hope your wishes all come true.
	I hope you find your pot of gold.

When you teach these allusions used in the examples, be sure the children are aware of the works of literature that they came from. If the phrase isn't one that most people recognize and one that comes from a familiar source, it doesn't really work as a literary allusion.

Remind the children that when they say or write things like, "Just Do It!" or "Don't worry, be happy," they are *alluding* to something that has been said or written that most people are familiar with. In that sense, these sayings are allusions. Readers will know the source and understand that the words are not original with the writer, but just to be on the safe side, they should use quotation marks to set the sayings apart from the rest of the text.

Extending the Lesson

— Call attention to literary illusion at every opportunity. Children will be surprised to find how many common sayings have their origins in famous works of literature, including the Bible, from famous quotations, speeches—both oral and written—and proverbs, fairy tales, and folk tales.

Mini-lesson 60
Say it with Symbols

Symbolism is nothing new to kids. From a very early age, they learn that golden arches mean McDonald's, red lights mean Stop and green lights mean Go, and a four-leaf clover stands for good luck. Symbolism in writing is an advanced extension of a familiar concept, but one children will need help in understanding. A few will be able to use symbolism successfully in their writing.

To help children better understand symbolism, use the words *stands for.* Ask what the American flag *stands for.* What does a smiley face or sticker on their paper *stand for?* Explain that writers often make a character or object in the story *stand for* a quality or something to be attained.

The best way to teach symbolism is within the context of stories the children love. For example:

The Little Red Hen is a symbol of industriousness.

A rainbow speaks of promise.

In *The Hundred Penny Box* by Sharon Mathis, each penny stands for a year in Aunt Dew's life.

C.S. Lewis, in his Christian allegory, *The Lion, the Witch, and the Wardrobe,* uses the Lion, Aslan, to depict Christ while the Witch stands for evil.

In the Uncle Remus stories, Brer Rabbit is the epitome of trickery, while in the *Tortoise and the Hare* tales, he stands for laziness.

Although understanding the concept of symbolism in writing may be difficult for young writers, they have no problem at all explaining what writing workshops stand for in their lives.

TIP

Again, this final mini-lesson is for awareness and to help students appreciate an author's intent.

Reproducibles
and
Transparency
Masters

Peer Conference Form

Writer's Name _____ Date _____

Title of Piece _____

I Heard You Say: _____

_____

_____

These are the things you did well: _____

_____

_____

_____

_____

These are things I noticed or that I want to know more about: _____

_____

_____

_____

_____

_____

_____

Conference Partner

This is what I will do as a result of this conference: _____

_____

_____

_____

_____

_____

Receiving Conference Form

Author _____ Title _____

Conference Partner _____ Date _____

In this piece I heard you say _____

_____

_____

_____

_____

_____

Writing Exciting Leads Peer Conference Form

Listen as each person in the group reads his/her piece. Check if the writer included where, when, and perhaps the time of day, in the setting, if the main character(s) is introduced, if there is some action (something happening), if the writer used some dialogue, and if the writer pulls you into the story and makes you want to read on.

Tell the writer what you like about the piece and suggest one way he/she might improve the piece.

After each member of the group has had an opportunity to share, make any changes that will improve your own piece of writing.

As a group, choose one person from your group to do a whole class sharing.

Reader #1	**Reader #2**	**Reader #3**
___ Setting	___ Setting	___ Setting
___ Character(s)	___ Character(s)	___ Character(s)
___ Action	___ Action	___ Action
___ Dialogue	___ Dialogue	___ Dialogue
___ Want to read on	___ Want to read on	___ Want to read on

Paragraph Power - The New-P, New-P Rule
Mini-lesson 38

New-P, New-P Rule
Narrative

New P-erson, New P-aragraph

New P-lace, New P-aragraph

New P-eriod of Time, New P-aragraph

New P-lot Event, New P-aragraph

New P-oint of View, New P-aragraph

New-P, New-P Rule
Expository

New P-iece, New-P-aragraph

New P-oint, New P-aragraph

New P-erson, New P-aragraph

New P-lace, New P-aragraph

New P-eriod of Time, New P-aragraph

Now P-ull It All Together, New P-aragraph

Ask Yourself These Questions As You Write

Title

Does my title fit my piece? Can the reader predict what my piece is about?

Lead

Does my lead "grab" the reader's attention? Does it make him want to read on?

Did I use a "hook"?

Information

Do I have enough information? Too much information?

Have I used examples?

Does my story have a setting: a time and place for the action to take place?

Did I tell my feelings?

Have I painted vivid word pictures for the reader?

Did I use sensory words?

Did I Show - Not Tell?

Is the information clear?

Was I specific?

Style

Did I use both long and short sentences?

Did I over-use any words (such as *and*, *said*, or *then*)?

Did I use paragraphs?

Is the information well organized? Is there a logical flow?

Did I use strong verbs?

Did I choose words carefully to say what I mean?

Did I keep the verb tense the same?

Does the voice stay the same — first person participant (I) or third person observer (he or she)?

Conclusion

Does my conclusion drop off? Is it too abrupt?

Does my conclusion drag on and on?

Is my conclusion logical?

Is my conclusion satisfying to the reader?

Fix Your Focus
Mini-lesson 6

Non-Example:

One of the most interesting people I know is my grandmother. She's my dad's mother and she isn't like any other grandmother you've ever known. She lives with my grandfather. He's interesting, too. He served in the Vietnam war. They live on a farm and raise llamas.

Example:

One of the most interesting people I know is my grandmother. She's my dad's mother and she isn't like any other grandmother you've ever known. She lives on a farm with my grandfather and raises llamas.

Exciting Leads
Mini-lesson 10

Non-example:

Once there was a Greek boy who wanted to come to America.

Example:

The setting sun spread a golden glow over the deserted market place. Twelve year old Tasso snatched his red flannel cap from his head as he darted down the cobblestone street. His legs, like pumping pistons, set the tassels of his loose knee-length trousers dancing. Suddenly Tasso stopped short. Loud excited voices from inside the coffeehouse drew him as a flame draws a moth.

From *Tasso of Tarpon Springs*

Non-example:

Omri got a weird birthday present.

Example:

It was not that Omri didn't appreciate Patrick's birthday present to him. Far from it. He was really very grateful — sort of. It was, without a doubt, very kind of Patrick to give Omri anything at all, let alone a secondhand plastic Indian that he himself had finished with.

From *The Indian in the Cupboard.* Lynne Reid Banks

Non-example:

This is a scary story about two kids who go into a spooky house on Halloween.

Example:

Jerry and Karyn's sneakers crunched the dry leaves on the path. "I don't know, Karyn," said Jerry, pushing his mask higher on his nose in order to see better. "It looks scary." Bare tree limbs cast shadows on the gray boards of the rickety old house. Its door, slightly ajar, creaked eerily on rusty hinges.

"Oh, come on Jerry. Don't be such a scairdy-cat," taunted Karyn. "Let's go in. After all, what could possibly happen?"

That's exactly what I'm worried about, thought Jerry.

Non-example:

Once our family went camping out west. It was a real adventure.

Example:

Mom and I unpacked the gear while Dad and Pete put up the tent. A sudden gust of cold wind sent shivers over my bare arms.

Mom tossed me a sweatshirt saying, "Even though it's August, it still gets cold this high in the mountains."

I smiled happily thinking to myself, "Our Rocky Mountain adventure has begun!"

Little did I know.

How to Write Exciting Narrative Leads
Mini-lesson 10

Writing an exciting lead can be compared to preparing for the opening act of a stage play. If the play (a story) is to be a hit, the writer needs to do these things:

Set the Stage:

> Hang the backdrop or scenery - let the reader know **when and where** the story is taking place.

> Use some props - **describe the setting** for the reader.

Bring the Actors on Stage:

> Introduce the **main characters.**

Let the Play Begin:

> Introduce some **action**; have the main character or characters do something. Let the actors interact; have the main characters begin talking; write some sparky **dialogue.**
>
> **Get the audience involved:** tease the reader and pull him into the story by posing a **problem** or suggesting a **conflict.**

How to Write Exciting Expository Leads
Mini-lesson 11

The purpose of an exciting expository lead is to "hook" the reader; to grab his attention and make him want to read on. Here are some ways to "hook" a reader:

Ask a question - Did you know that Australia is called "The Land Down Under?"

Make a startling statement - Kangaroos are road kill in Australia!

Quick visual images - Kangaroos! A laughing kookaburra! Sleepy wombats and howling dingos!

A Challenge - I'll bet you can't think of a single place that has more unusual animals than Australia.

Fascinating facts - Kangaroos can grow to be six feet tall. Even though they weigh about 200 pounds, they can leap up to 25 feet in just one hop. They can run as fast as 30 miles an hour!

Personal anecdote or feeling - My friend, Jim, moved to Australia. He sends me e-mail often telling me about his new home in the Land Down Under. Each one I receive makes me want to see this fascinating land for myself.

Satisfying Endings
Mini-lesson 12

Non-example:

And that's all I have to say.

Example:

Mariah waved as long as she thought he could still see her, then watched as the line of Indians grew faint in the distance. She remembered Daddie calling the removal of the Indians to the West the Trail of Tears. Today, the trail was theirs once more, but the tears were her own.

Non-example:

That's the end of my story. "Bye now."

Example:

As Dad put the last of the gear into the van, I stood quietly gazing at the majestic mountains. I wanted to memorize every detail. Our Rocky Mountain Adventure was over. We were going home.

Non-example:

I hope you learned something about wood storks.

Example:

Now that you've learned about where wood storks live, what and how they eat, why they're important, and how they be came an endangered species, I hope you, too, will want to help protect these fascinating birds.

How to Write Satisfying Narrative Endings
Mini-lesson 12

A well-written narrative has a solid ending that demonstrates the story is over and gives the narrative a sense of completeness. Young writers can achieve this in their writing by answering one or more of the following questions in concluding their narrative.

1. How did you (or the main character) feel about the experience?

2. What did you (or the main character) learn from the experience?

3. Would you want anyone else to have the same experience?

4. What would you (or the main character) do differently?

5. Would you (or the main character) want to repeat the experience?

6. If there was a problem, how was the problem solved?

7. If there was a conflict, how was the conflict resolved?

8. How have you (or the main character) changed as a result of the experience?

How to Write Satisfying Expository Endings
Mini-lesson 12

A solid expository ending will tie all the information together and leave the reader with a sense of completeness. Although the reader may want to do some further research into the topic, the piece itself should not have unanswered questions.

Here are some ways to end an expository piece:

Summary of the main points - write a brief summary of the main points you made, using words like: *For all these reasons. . . In conclusion. . .* you can see why conservation is important to all of us.

Evaluative statement - Conservation is an important issue for all Americans. . .

Challenge - The next time you are tempted to throw trash. . .

Feelings - I personally feel that it is every American's duty to practice conservation.

Value to the reader statement - The information I've presented will help you to practice better conservation and help you convince others to conserve our resources.

Invitation - Wouldn't you like to be part of the effort to conserve our resources?

Further exploration - If you'd like to know more about. . .

Restatement - My purpose in writing was to convince you that conservation is an important issue in our country.

Build Bridges
Mini-lesson 13

Non-example:

Our teacher, Mrs. Grinch, gave us fifty long division problems for homework. I had to practice the piano after school. Then we had a soccer game right after dinner. It was really late when the game ended, so I didn't have time to do the problems.

Mrs. Grinch said, "The first person in each row will collect the homework."

Example:

Our teacher, Mrs. Grinch, gave us 50 long division problems for homework. I had to practice the piano after school. Then we had a soccer game right after dinner. It was really late when the game ended, so I didn't have time to do the problems.

The next day, Mrs. Grinch said, "The first person in each row will collect the homework."

Non-example:

While Natalie and Jordan were playing pick-up sticks, Natalie's little brother, Davy, snuck up behind them and yelled, "I want to play, too!" causing Natalie to move a stick and miss her turn.

"Get out of here and leave us alone!" shouted Natalie.

Hearing the commotion from the kitchen, Natalie's mom called out, "Natalie, be nice to your little brother."

The girls sat on Natalie's bed planning how to get even.

Example:

While Jordan and Natalie were playing pick-up sticks, Natalie's little brother snuck up behind them and yelled, "I want to play, too!" causing Natalie to move a stick and miss her turn.

"Get out of here and leave us alone," shouted Natalie.

Hearing the commotion from the kitchen, Natalie's mom called in to them, "Natalie, be nice to your little brother."

Later, in Natalie's bedroom, the girls sat on Natalie's bed planning how to get even.

Non-example:

Reading is my favorite subject. I like to read because I can learn about many different places. I loved reading about the Swiss Alps in the book <u>Heidi.</u> Reading makes dull days exciting.

Example:

Reading is my favorite subject. I like to read because I can learn about many different places. I loved reading about the Swiss Alps in the book <u>Heid</u>i.
Another reason I like to read is because reading makes dull days exciting.

Non-example:

 I also like to read because I can go on adventures with the main characters in the books. So now you know why I like to read.

Example:

I also like to read because I can go on adventures with the main characters in the books.
For all these reasons: because I can learn about new places, make dull days exciting, and go on adventures with the main characters, reading is one of my favorite things to do.

Write for Your Reader
Mini-lesson 14

Sarah's Story

Non-example:

Drip castles is dry sand and you get water and put wet sand then take some wet sand out and drip it on the dry sand and get it real tall and then you've got it!

Example:

Make a pile of sand on the beach. Then go down to the ocean, and get water in a bucket. Now put sand in the bucket, not from the pile, but from the sand that is extra. Now take a handful of the wet sand and put it on the pile of sand. Get it tall, then you've got it!

Non-example:

We were playing tether-ball at recess. While I waited for my turn, I talked with my friend, Susan. The next thing I knew, he smacked the ball so hard it came off the rope. Whack! It hit me on the side of my head.

Example:

We were playing tether-ball at recess. While I was waiting for my turn, and talking with my friend Susan, Jimmy stepped in to play. The next thing I knew, he smacked the ball so hard it came off the rope. Whack! The ball hit me on the side of my head.

Non-example:

Mom and I held hands tightly as we waited on the corner. Cars seemed to be rushing at us from every direction. Horns tooted. He blew his shrill whistle. People hurried by.

Example:

Mom and I held hands tightly as we waited on the corner of Fifth Avenue, the busiest street in New York City. Cars seemed to be rushing at us from every direction. Horns tooted. A policeman blew his shrill whistle. People hurried by.

Non-example:

Dad blew his stack when he got home. He took one look at it and started yelling, "I can't believe you did this again!"

Example:

Dad blew his stack when he got home. He took one look at my mangled bike and started yelling, "I can't believe you did this again!"

Non-example:

This is how you do it. You take one piece and spread it with peanut cover. Then cover it with jelly. Then put another piece on top. Enjoy.

Example:

This is how you make a peanut butter and jelly sandwich. First, spread one piece of bread with a layer of peanut butter. Then spread a layer of jelly over the peanut butter. Put another slice of bread on top of the first slice. Enjoy!

Paragraph Power
Mini-lesson 38

Non-example:

Mom's voice rang out from the kitchen. "Hurry up, Chip, you'll be late for school. I pulled on my jeans with the grass stain on the knee from the day I slid into home and dug my dirty sweat shirt out of the laundry basket. It had a big chocolate splotch on the front and was pretty wrinkled. Then I dropped my lucky marble in my pocket. I was ready. When I went into the kitchen, my stomach lurched. Mom was cooking oatmeal. I hate oatmeal! Five minutes later, after I had covered the oatmeal with brown sugar and drowned the whole mess in milk, I was able to swallow it down without gagging too much. Then I bolted out the door before Mom could yell at me for wearing dirty clothes to school. Joey was already at the bus stop. He can be a real pain. He's also my best friend. His silly grin made me feel a lot better. But not for long, "Hey, Chip," he said, "where's your backpack?"

Example:

Mom's voice rang out from the kitchen, "Hurry up, Chip, you'll be late for school."

I pulled on my jeans with the grass stain on the knee from the day I slid into home and dug my dirty sweat shirt out of the laundry basket. It had a big chocolate splotch on the front and was pretty wrinkled. Then I dropped my lucky marble in my pocket. I was ready.

When I went into the kitchen, my stomach lurched. Mom was cooking oatmeal. I hate oatmeal! But after I had covered the oatmeal with brown sugar and drowned the whole mess in milk, I was able to swallow it down without gagging too much.

Then I bolted out the door before Mom could yell at me for wearing dirty clothes to school.

Joey was already at the bus stop. He can be a real pain. He's also my best friend. His silly grin made me feel a lot better. But not for long.

"Hey, Chip," he said, "where's your backpack?"

Paragraph Power
Mini-lesson 38

(new piece)   Cars! Trains! Planes! Even cruise ships! There are lots of ways to travel. But if I had my choice, I'd choose planes every time.

(new period of time)   Last year I flew for the very first time to Kansas to visit my grandparents. I had a blast and knew then that flying would forever be my favorite way to travel. It was so much fun, I didn't want the plane to land even though I was glad to see my grandma and grandpa.

(new point)   Flying is fast and, for someone like me who is impatient, that's important. The last time we went to Kansas, we went by car. I thought we'd never get there! It took five whole days of driving, driving, driving. By plane the whole trip only took three hours. I didn't have time to get restless.

(new person)   Of course, my Mom said I should have enjoyed the scenery from the windows of the car. But I said, "How many wheat fields can one person enjoy seeing?"

(new point)   Speaking of seeing, that's another thing great about flying. I loved looking out the window at the midget cars and doll houses far below us. Rivers looked like brown ribbons and swimming pools seemed to be the size of postage stamps. The world looks totally different from way up in the sky.

(new point)   Another neat thing about flying is that the stewardesses bring food to you. There's a cute little tray that pulls down from the back of the seat in front of you to use while you're eating. I'm not saying it's the best food in the world, but it sure beats starving to death while you wait for your Dad to decide to stop for gas or a lunch break! On the flight to Kansas, we had little turkey sandwiches, individual bags of chips, applesauce, a chocolate chip cookie, and fruit juice.

(new place)   When we landed in Kansas City the airport was a beehive of activity. Flying is exciting because there's so much to see and do at the airport. People rushing to catch their flights, planes coming in and going out, and announcements over the loud speakers made my head spin!

(pull it all together)   Yes, the speed of flights, the fun of observing the world from on high, the novelty of eating airline food from little trays, and the excitement of airports all convince me that flying is the only way to go!

Paragraph Power
Mini-lesson 38

Non-example:

The first step when you are doing a research report is to choose the topic. Not only is this the first step, it may well be the most important one. Choosing your topic well can make the difference between a finished report that is interesting to read and one that is only ho-hum. Choose a topic that is interesting to you. If you are not interested in the subject, it will be very hard to write a report that is enjoyable for others to read.

Example:

The first step when you are doing a research report is to choose the topic. Not only is this the first step, it may well be the most important one. Choosing your topic well can make the difference between a finished report that is interesting to read and one that is only ho-hum.

Choose a topic that is interesting to you If you are not interested in the subject, it will be very hard to write a report that is enjoyable for others to read.

Weed That Garden!
Mini-lesson 39

Non-example:

It was chilly that last day in March. So I put on my jacket and headed for school. And on the way, I saw something sparkling in the grass beside the road. So I picked it up. And it was a diamond! Then I looked all around to see if anyone was looking for it. And no one was. So then I didn't know quite what to do. Then I dropped the diamond into my shirt pocket. And then I went to school.

Example:

It was chilly that last day in March. I put on my jacket and headed for school. On the way, I saw something sparkling in the grass beside the road. I picked it up. It was a diamond! I looked all around to see if anyone was looking for it. No one was. I didn't know quite what to do. I dropped the diamond into my shirt pocket and went on to school.

T.E.S.S.
Mini-lesson 41

T-ell your idea.

E-xplain the idea.

S-upport the idea with a detail

S-upport the idea with an example

Of course, you can add on more S's! For a paragraph choosing a favorite place to visit, T.E.S.S. might look like this:

T - I'd love to visit Australia to see the unusual animals that live there.

E - Australia has all kinds of animals that don't live in the United States. Because Australia is an island, animals there are different from ones found other places. I'd love to see them in their native habitat.

S - I'd give anything to see kangaroos in the outback, wombats burrowing long tunnels at night, koala bears feeding in a eucalyptus tree, or a bird that can't fly, the emu.

S - Animals in Australia sure are different. My friend, Jim, says that in Australia, kangaroos are road kill! And he ought to know, because he lives there.

Keep 'em in Suspense!
Mini-lesson 49

Jonas' heart swelled with gratitude and pride. But at the same time he was filled with fear. He did not know what his selection meant. He did not know what he was to become. Or what would become of him.

From *The Giver,* by Lois Lowry

"Help!" cried the Centipede.

"Save us!" cried Miss Spider.

"We are lost!" cried the Ladybug.

"This is the end!" cried the Old-Green-Grasshopper.

"James!" cried the Earthworm. "Do something, James! Quickly, do something!"

"I can't!" cried James. "I'm sorry! Good-bye! Shut your eyes everybody! It won't be long now!"

From *James and the Giant Peach* by Roald Dahl

Surprise Your Reader!
Mini-lesson 55

Clutching her panther claw, Mariah moved on. A rat snake slithered across the path in front of her. Mariah clenched her teeth. A cold chill ran over her body. A few steps more. Splat! Something cold and wet landed on her cheek. Brushing it off frantically, the thing plopped in front of her. A tree frog! It was nothing but a tree frog.

From: *Panther Girl*

Author and/or Illustrator Videos

Eric Carle: Picture Writer. New York: Scholastic Inc., 1993

Good Conversation! A Talk with Jane Yolen. Scarborough, NY, Tim Podell Productions, P.O. Box 244, Scarborough, NY 10510

The World of Norman Bridwell Featuring Clifford, the Big Red Dog. New York: Scholastic, 1990

Riding the Magic School Bus with Joanna Cole and Bruce Degen. New York: Scholastic, 1992.

Beatrix Potter: Artist, Storyteller and Countrywoman, Scholastic.

Getting to Know William Steig, Scholastic.

Take Joy!: The Magic World of Tasha Tudor, Scholastic.

A Visit with Rosemary Wells, Scholastic.

A Visit with Tomie DePaola, Scholastic.

Tomie DePaola Live in Concert, Scholastic.

Recommended for Your Professional Library

Calkins, Lucy McCormick. *Lessons From a Child - On the Teaching and Learning of Writing.* New Hampshire: Heinemann Educational Books, 1983.

Copperud, Roy H. *American Usage and Style The Consensus.* New York:Van Nostrand Reinhold Company, 1980.

Danish, Barbara. *Writing as a Second Language: A Workbook for Writing and Teaching Writing.* New York: Teachers&Writers, 1981.

Forney, Melissa. *The Writing Menu: Ensuring Success for Every Student.* Gainesville: Maupin House Publishing, 1999.

Freeman, Marcia S. *Building a Writing Community: A Practical Guide.* Gainesville: Maupin House Publishing, 1995.

Graves, Donald H. *Writing: Teachers & Children At Work.* New Hampshire: Heinemann Educational Books, 1983.

Graves, Donald H. *Experiment With Fiction: The Reading/Writing Teacher's Companion.* New Hampshire, Heinemann Educational Books, 1989.

Graves, Donald H. *Discover Your Own Literacy. The Reading/Writing Teacher's Companion.* New Hampshire: Heinemann Educational Books, 1990.

Graves, Donald H. *Build a Literate Classroom.* New Hampshire: Heinemann Educational Books, 1991.

Graves, Donald H. *A Fresh Look at Writing.* New Hampshire: Heinemann Educational Books, 1994.

Trost, Mary Ann & Editorial Staff. *Teaching and Evaluating Student Writing.* Illinois: McDougal, Littell & Company, 1985.

Murray, Donald. *Writing for Your Readers: Notes on the Writer's Craft from The Boston Globe.* Connecticut.: The Globe Pequot Press, 1983.

Peck, Robert Newton. *Fiction is Folks.* Ohio: Writer's Digest Books, 1983.

Proett, Jackie and Gill, Kent. *The Writing Process in Action: A Handbook for Teachers.* Illinois: National Council of Teachers of English, 1986.

Zinsser, William. *On Writing Well.* New York: Harper & Row Publishers, 1980.

Bibliography

Mini-lesson 1 - Put Muscles in Your Verbs
Schiller, Andrew & Jenkins, William A. *In Other Words: A Beginning Thesaurus.* New York: Lothrop, Lee, and Shepard Company, 1978.
Urdang, Laurence. *A Basic Dictionary of Synonyms and Antonyms.* New York: Elsevier/ Nelson Books, 1978.
Witels, Harriet & Greisman, Joan. *The Clear and Simple Thesaurus Dictionary.* New York: Grosset & Dunlap, 1971.
Witels, Harriet & Greisman, Joan. *A First Thesaurus.* New York: Golden Book, 1985.

Mini-lesson 3 - Tell It All.
Christelow, Eileen. *What Do Authors Do?* New York: Clarion Books, 1995.
Fitzpatrick, Marie-Louise. *The Long March.* Oregon: Beyond Words Publishing, Inc., 1998.
Schrecengost, Maity. *Write to Be Read.* Wisconsin: Alleyside Press, 1972.
Tresselt, Alvin. *White Snow, Bright Snow.* New York: Lothrop, Lee & Shepard Co., 1947.
Van Allsburg, Chris. *Jumanji.* Boston: Houghton Mifflin Company, 1981.

Mini-lesson 5 - Paint Vivid Word Pictures.
Adams, Jeanie. *Going for Oysters.* Illinois: Albert Whitman & Company, 1991.
Auch, Mary Jane. *I Was a Third Grade Science Project.* New York: Holiday House, 1998.
Schrecengost, Maity. *Write to Be Read.* Wisconsin: Alleyside Press, 1972.

Mini-lesson 6 - Fix Your Focus.
Christelow, Eileen. *What Do Authors Do?* New York: Clarion Books, 1995.
Roderman, Winifred Ho. *Writing 1: Getting Started.* California: Fearon/Janus, 1990.
Schrecengost, Maity. *Write to Be Read.* Wisconsin: Alleyside Press, 1992.

Mini-lesson 7 - Show - Don't Tell.
Byers, Betsy. *Wanted . . .Mud Blossom.* New York: Delacort Press, 1991.
Ferris, Jeri. *Go Free or Die A Story about Harriet Tubman.* Minnesota: Carolrhoda Books, 1988.
Schrecengost, Maity. *Write to Be Read.* Wisconsin: Alleyside Press, 1992.

Mini-lesson 8 - Lights! Camera! Action!
Burch, Robert. *Ida Early Comes Over the Mountain.* New York: Viking Press, 1980.
Elliott, Leslee. *Really Radical Reptiles.* New York: Sterling Publishing Co., Inc., 1994.

Mini-lesson 9 - Set the Scene.
Baum, L. Frank. *The Wizard of Oz.* New York: William Morrow & Co, 1987 Edition.
Brink, Carol Ryrie. *Caddie Woodlawn.* New York: Simon & Schuster, 1983.
de Angeli, Marguerite. *The Door in the Wall.* New York: Doubleday Books Reissue, 1989.
O'Dell, Scott. *Island of the Blue Dolphins.* Boston: Houghton Mifflin Company, 1950, 1988.
Speare, Elizabeth George. *The Witch of Blackbird Pond.* New York: Houghton Mifflin Company, 1958.

Mini-lesson 10 - Exciting Leads

Avi. *Sore Losers*. New York: Avon Books, 1984.

Banks, Lynne Reid. *The Indian in the Cupboard.* New York: Avon Books, 1980.

Keehn, Sally. *I Am Regina*. New York: Bantam Doubleday Books for Young Readers, 1991.

Paulson, Gary. *My Life in Dog Years*. New York: Bantam Doubleday Books for Young Readers, 1998.

Robinson, Barbara. *The Best Christmas Pageant Ever*. New York: HarperCollins, 1972.

Schrecengost, Maity. *Tasso of Tarpon Springs*. Gainesville:Maupin House Publishing Inc., 1998.

Mini-lesson 11 - Grab Your Reader's Attention!

Cobblestone. Peterborough, NH: Cobblestone Publishing Company.

ContactKids. New York: Sesame Workshop.

Elliott, Leslee. *Really Radical Reptiles and Amphibians*. Sterling Publishing Co., Inc. ,1994.

National Geographic World. Washington, DC:National Geographic Society.

Odyssey Adventures in Science. Petersborough: Cobblestone Publishing Com Company.

Ranger Rick. Virginia: National Wildlife Federation.

Mini-lesson 12 - Satisfying Endings.

Babbitt, Natalie. *Knee-knock Rise*. New York: Scholastic, 1970.

Dahl, Roald. *Charlie and the Great Glass Elevator*. New York: Alfred A. Knopf, 1972.

Fleischman, Paul. *The Half-a-Moon-Inn*. New York: Scholastic, 1980.

Paulsen, Gary. *Hatchet*. New York: Simon & Schuster, 1987.

Schrecengost, Maity. *Panther Girl*. Gainesville: Maupin House Publishing, Inc., 1999.

White, E.B. *Charlotte's Web*. New York: Harper and Row, 1952.

Williams, Margery. *The Velveteen Rabbit*. New York: Holt, Rinehart and Winston, 1983.

Cobblestone. Peterborough, NH: Cobblestone Publishing Company.

ContactKids. New York: Sesame Workshop.

Elliott, Leslee. *Really Radical Reptiles and Amphibians*. Sterling Publishing Co., Inc. , 1994.

National Geographic World. Washington, DC:National Geographic Society.

Odyssey Adventures in Science. Petersborough: Cobblestone Publishing Com Company.

Ranger Rick. Virginia: National Wildlife Federation.

Mini-lesson 14 - Write for Your Reader.

Christelow, Eileen. *What Do Authors Do?* New York: Clarion Books, 1995.

Schrecengost, Maity. *Write to Be Read*. Wisconsin: Alleyside Press, 1992.

Mini-lesson 15 - Variety Adds the Spice.

Bunting, Eve. *Nasty Stinky Sneakers*. New York: HarperCollins Publishers, 1994.

Stein, R. Conrad. *The Story of the Flight at Kitty Hawk*. Chicago: Children's Press, 1981.

Mini-lesson 16 - S-t-r-e-t-c-h a Sentence.

Heller, Ruth. *Many Luscious Lollipops A Book About Adjectives*. New York: Grosset and Dunlap, 1989.

Heller, Ruth. *Up, Up and Away: A Book About Adverbs*. New York: Grosset and Dunlap, 1991.

Roderman, Winifred Ho. *Writing 1:Getting Started*. CA: Fearon, Janus, 1990.

Mini-lesson 17 - Crunch Sentences.

Roderman, Winifred Ho. *Writing 1: Getting Started*. Fearon, Janus, 1990.

Mini-lesson 18 - Bring Your Characters to Life.

Dahl, Roald. *Danny, The Champion of the World*. New York: Puffin Books, 1988.

Dahl, Roald. *Matilda*. New York: Viking Press, 1988.

Lindgren, Astrid. *Pippi Longstocking*. New York: Puffin Books, 1997.

Parish, Peggy. *Amelia Bedelia*. New York: HarperCollins Juvenile Books, 1992.

Mini-lesson 19-23 - Give Your Characters Person-ality.

MacLachlan, Patricia. *Sarah Plain and Tall*. New York: Harper & Row Publishers, 1985.

O'Dell, Scott. *The Black Pearl*. New York: Dell Publishing, 1967.

Schrecengost, Maity. *Write to Be Read*. Wisconsin: Alleyside Press, 1992.

Wojciechowska, Maia. *Shadow of a Bull*. New York: Atheneum, 1974.

Mini-lesson 24 - What's In a Name?
Dahl, Roald. *Charlie and the Chocolate Factory*. New York: Alfred Knopf, 1985.
Greenwald, Sheila. *Here's Hermione. A Rosy Cole Production*. Boston: Little, Brown and Company, 1991.
Havill, Juanita. *It Always Happens to Leona*. New York: Crown Publishers, 1989.
Lindgren, Astrid. *Pippi Longstocking*. New York: Puffin Books, 1997.
Milne. A.A. *The Best of Winnie -the -Pooh*. USA: Penquin Books, 1997.

Mini-lesson 25 - Try Tags.
Peck, Robert Newton. *Soup*. New York: Knopf Edition, 1998.

Mini-lesson 26 - Let the Reader See What You See.
O'Neill, Catherine. *You Won't Believe Your Eyes*. Washington, DC: National Geographic, 1987.

Mini-lesson 27 - Smell What You Smell.
Moncure, Jane Belk. *What Your Nose Knows*. Chicago: Children's Press, 1982.

Mini-lesson 28 - Hear What You Hear.
Moncure, Jane Belk. *Sounds All Around*. Chicago: Children's Press, 1982.

Mini-lesson 30 - Feel What You Feel.
Otto, Carolyn. *I Can Tell by Touching*. New York: HarperCollins Publishers, 1994.

Mini-lesson 31 - Put Them All Together
McMillan, Bruce. *Sense Surprise: A Guessing Game for the Five Senses*. New York: Scholastic, 1994.

Mini-lesson 32 - Mood Magic
Fleischman, Paul. *Rondo in C*. New York: Harper & Row, 1988.
Sommer, Elyse. *The Kids' World Almanac of Music from Rock to Bach*. New York: Pharos Books, 1991.

Mini-lessons 33-37 - Show Your Character's Feelings
Aliki. *Feelings*. New York: Greenwillow Books, 1984.
Arnos, Janine. A series of books on feelings: *Hurt, Jealous, Lonely, Sad, Afraid*. US: Steck-Vaughn Company, 1991.

Mini-lesson 40 - Support Your Great Ideas.
Buckley, Helen E. *Moonlight Kite*. New York: Lothrop, Lee & Shepard Books, 1997.
Lamar, William W. *The World's Most Spectacular Reptiles & Amphibians*. Tampa: World Publications, 1997.

Mini-lesson 41 - Examples Give Extra Support.
Betz, Adrienne. *Scholastic Treasury of Quotations for Children*. New York: Scholastic, 1998.
Bitton-Jackson, Livia. *I Have Lived a Thousand Years: Growing Up in the Holocaust*. New York: Scholastic, Inc., 1997.
Freedman, Russell. *Indian Chiefs*. New York: Scholastic Inc., 1987.
Senn, J.A. *Quotations for Kids*. Connecticut: The Millbrook Press 1999.

Mini-lesson 42 - Get Real!
Avi. *What Do Fish Have to Do with Anything?* Mass: Candlewick Press, 1997.
Dahl, Roald. *James and the Giant Peach*. New York: Alfred A. Knopf,1961.
Harris Joel Chandler. *The Complete Tales of Uncle Remus*. New York: Houghton Mifflin, Co., 1955.
Lenski, Lois. *Strawberry Girl*. New York: Dell Publishing, 1945, 1973.

Mini-lesson 43 - Sensational Similes
Hanson, Joan. *Similes: As Gentle As a Lamb, Spin Like a Top*. Jane Hanson Word Books.
Juster, Norman. *As Silly as Knees, As Busy As Bees. An Astounding Assortment of Similes*. New York: Econo-Clad Books, 1999.
Juster, Norman. *A Surfeit of Similes*. New York: Morrow Junior Books, 1989.

Mini-lesson 44 - Magnificent Metaphors.
Tester, Sylvia Root. *You Dance Like An Ostrich*. Harvest Booksearch, 1978.

Mini-lesson 46 - Get Noisy with Onomatopoeia

DeZutter, Hank. *Who Says a Dog Goes Bow-Wow?* New York: Stewart, Tabor and Chang, 1993.

Robinson, Marc. *Cock-a-Doodle-Doo!* New York: Doubleday Books for Young Readers, 1993.

Mini-lesson 47 - Alluring Alliteration

Kellogg, Steven. *Aster Aardvark's Alphabet Adventures.* New York: William Morrow and Company, Inc., 1987.

Heller, Nicholas. *Goblins in Green.* New York: Greenwillow Books, 1995.

Mini-lesson 48 - Don't Keep the Reader in the Dark!

Avi. *The True Confessions of Charlotte Doyle.* New York: Orchard Books, 1990.

Fleischman, Paul. *The Half-A-Moon Inn.* New York: Scholastic Inc., 1980.

O'Dell, Scott. *The Black Pearl.* New York: Dell Publishing, 1967.

Mini-lesson 49 - Keep 'em in Suspense!

Banks, Lynne Reid. *Indian in the Cupboard.* New York: Avon Books, 1980.

Bulla, Clyde Robert. *A Lion to Guard Us.* New York: Harper Trophy Reissue Edition, 1989.

Dahl, Roald. *Charlie and the Great Glass Elevator.* New York: Alfred A. Knopf, Inc., 1972.

Pierce, Tamora. *Alanna: The First Adventure.* New York: Random House, 1989.

Mini-lesson 50 - Use a Little Hype!

Osborne, Mary Pope. *American Tall Tales.* New York: Alfred A. Knopf, 1991.

San Souci, Robert D. *Larger than Life. The Adventures of American Legendary Heroes.* New York: Doubleday Books for Young Readers, 1991.

Mini-lesson 51 -Say It With Meaning!

Dahl, Roald. *Charlie and the Chocolate Factory.* New York: Alfred Knopf, 1985.

Mini-lesson 52 - An Anthropomorphic Angle.

Harris, Joel Chandler. *Complete Tales of Uncle Remus.* New York: Houghton Mifflin Co., 1955.

Lawson, Robert. *Rabbit Hill.* New York: Puffin Books, 1944, 1972.

Leaf, Murro. *The Story of Ferdinand.* New York:Viking Press, 1987.

Lobel, Arnold. *Fables.* New York: Harper & Row Publishers, 1980.

O'Brien, Robert. *Mrs. Frisby and the Rats of NIMH.* New York: Atheneum, 1974.

Silverstein, Shel. *The Giving Tree.* New York: HarperCollins Juvenile Books, 1986.

Mini-lesson 53 - Bring Things to Life.

L'Engle, Madeleine. *A Wrinkle in Time.* New York, Yearling Books (Reissue), 1997.

Lewis, C. S. *The Lion, the Witch, and the Wardrobe.* New York: Macmillan Publishing Company, 1950.

Young, Ed. *Lon PoPo.* New York: Philomel Books, 1989.

Mini-lesson 54 - Try a Rhyme.

Larrick, Nancy. *When the Dark Comes Dancing: A Bedtime Poetry Book.* New York: Philomel Books, 1983.

Yolen, Jane, Editor. *Street Rhymes Around the World.* Honesdale, PA: Wordsong Boyd's Mill Press, 1992.

Mini-lesson 55 - Surprise Your Reader!

Dahl, Roald. *Danny The Champion of the World.* New York: Puffin Books, 1975.

Mini-lesson 56 - Could You Repeat That?

Aardema, Verna. *Why Mosquitoes Buzz in People's Ears.* New York: Dial Press, 1975.

Mini-lesson 57 - Color Your Dialogue with Colloquialisms

Cassidy, Frederic G. Chief Ed. *Dictionary of American Regional English.* MA: HarvardUniversity Press, 1985.

Mini-lesson 58 - Season Your Dialogue with Idioms!

Cox, James A. *Put Your Foot in Your Mouth.* New York: Random House, 1980.

Terban, Marvin. *Mad as a Wet Hen.* New York: Clarion Books, 1987.

Terban, Marvin. *Punching the Clock.* New York: Clarion Books, 1990.

Terban, Marvin. *Scholastic Dictionary of Idioms.* New York: Scholastic, 1998.

About the Author

Maity Schrecengost is an author and former classroom teacher. She now appears at schools for author visits to receive what says is her "oxygen"—contact with children! She also conducts inservice workshops for classroom teachers, specializing in helping teachers teach elaboration and writing craft.

Educated in public schools in a small town in southwestern Pennsylvania, Maity earned her BA from Allegheny College. After marriage and teaching a few years, she took time off to raise two children, Lynda and Tom, before resuming her teaching career. Shortly after returning to teaching, Maity had the good fortune to sit at the feet of writing guru, Donald Graves, for several years in preparation for becoming one of a cadre of teachers involved in the Pennsylvania Department of Education Writing Project. In that capacity, Maity presented writing workshops throughout the state of Pennsylvania.

After a move to Florida in 1986, while teaching in a public school, she began to pursue her personal writing career with a focus on writing historical fiction and educational books for young readers.

Maity holds a Master's degree in English from NOVA University.